from front flap

migrant in fiction. Carlton C. Qualey, chairman of the department of history at Carleton College, contributes two essays. In the first he surveys world population movements and in the second he suggests new source materials for immigration studies. Henry A. Pochmann, professor of American literature at the University of Wisconsin, discusses the migration of ideas — what ideas have come into America, from where, and to what end? Franklin D. Scott, professor of history at Northwestern University, inquires into the value of immigration studies of nationality groups. The Reverend Colman J. Barry, associate professor of history at St. John's University, Collegeville, Minnesota, explores possibilities for future immigration studies. Theodore C. Blegen, dean emeritus of the University of Minnesota graduate school, takes a backward glance and a forward look at immigration studies.

The volume is based on the papers given at a conference held at the University of Minnesota in honor of Dr. Blegen on his retirement from the university.

IMMIGRATION AND AMERICAN HISTORY

*Based on a Conference at the University of
Minnesota, January 29–30, 1960*

THEODORE C. BLEGEN

Immigration
AND AMERICAN HISTORY

Essays in Honor of Theodore C. Blegen

EDITED BY HENRY STEELE COMMAGER

University of Minnesota Press, Minneapolis

Foreword

IN THAT nostalgic recollection of his boyhood on Lake Minnetonka, "The Saga of Saga Hill," Theodore Blegen tells us how his father used to greet the Blegen boys, morning after morning, with the robust admonition: "Boys, this is a working day." He tells us, too, how he and his brothers learned to outwit parental supervision, but the fact is that the habit of regarding each day as a working day sank in very deeply. And what prodigies of work Dean Blegen has performed.

There was the Minnesota State Historical Society which he took over; he made it, and its lively quarterly magazine, the envy of other states. He persuaded local historical groups all over the state to ferret out source material to load the shelves of the society's great library, and within a short time the whole state was ablaze with historical enthusiasm. To satisfy this state-wide appetite for history, he then contributed a series of Minnesota histories for every age group. It might be said, without much exaggeration, that the driving force that led Hawaii and Alaska to seek statehood was the realization that it was worth while being a state if you could get a Blegen to write your history.

One job has never been enough to engage the whole of his torrential energies, and he took on the Norwegian-American Historical Association at the same time that he was superintending the whole of Minnesota history, made it a model of what such an organization should be, and sponsored an invaluable collection of historical studies and translations — many of them his own — running to some forty volumes. Even more important than these

editorial activities are the great scholarly works which he has somehow found time to write. It would be an exaggeration to say that
he pioneered in opening up the field of immigration, but no exaggeration to say that no one has contributed more to the cultivation
of that field. And all the while he has presided as dean of a swarm-
ing graduate school.

An autobiographical sketch which Theodore Blegen contributed
some years ago to *Minnesota Writes* is modest enough, but it
yields, through what our literary colleagues call an *explication du
texte*, a rich insight into his character. What is most striking is
least calculated: the vocabulary itself. "I had fun," he begins, "trying to enlist the aid of the people of Minnesota," and "I had the
pleasure of publishing Sibley's Autobiography," and again, "one of
the delights of historical research . . . the magic of diaries and
other documents." This choice of words is not fortuitous. One of
Dean Blegen's signal contributions — surely in a teacher and a dean
an inspired one — is that he has always brought zest and happiness
to the work of education and of scholarship. At a time when so
much of our scholarship — even our historical scholarship — is ex-
cessively solemn and painfully impersonal, and when so many
young scholars think it necessary to present their findings in a language drained of color or of passion, he has emphasized the pleas-
ures of scholarship. He has brought to the study of history much
of his own sense of excitement, his own delight in the richness of
the intellectual life, his own resounding Yes to all the demands and
the challenges of life.

There is another quality in Dean Blegen's historical writing,
closely connected with this feeling of excitement which he com-
municates: that is the sense of drama and of a story, in all his
writing. Today historians hold solemn conferences, or wakes, to
lament the passing of the popularity of history: why do the young
so generally dislike history; why do their elders almost invariably
choose other than historical volumes for serious reading? It was
not ever thus — we are reminded — not in the days when Prescott
and Motley adorned every parlor table, and avid readers rioted in
bookshops for Macaulay's latest volume. One of the reasons, per-

haps the primary reason, for the declining popularity of history is that historians have themselves lost interest in it. At least they have almost stopped trying to tell a story. They have turned history into a series of sociological analyses, or of problems, and this at every level, so that even the little innocents who come to us hopefully for a story are fobbed off with a series of headaches: not the Pilgrim Fathers but the Problem of Colonial Settlement; not Paul Revere but the Problem of the Revolution; not Daniel Boone or Lewis and Clark but the Problem of the Westward Movement and the Problem of the Public Lands; not even Jacob Riis and the Making of an American, but the Problem of Immigrant Adjustment.

Dean Blegen has always had a lively sense for history as an unfolding story, and for history as people. In his histories something is always happening; his people are not statistical items, but poor Norwegian fishermen or cotters who sing mournful ballads, or Minnesota farmer-wives painfully writing letters home to the old country, or boys and girls in icy churches listening piously to sermons that no longer have meaning to them. Theodore Blegen has the same feeling for history that animated Ole Rölvaag and Johan Bojer, the same interest in the poor and the forgotten, the women and children, the plain people with their hopes and disappointments, their concern for the weather and the crops, for school and church, their quiet pride in their new homes, their deep sadness for what they have given up, their endless wonder at what life has done to them and what it promises to do to their children in this New World.

There is a third quality in Dean Blegen's work that has implications for education and scholarship. I refer to his habit — a habit so deeply ingrained that it is instinctive — of beginning with the particular and moving on from it to the general, rather than taking refuge in the general or in generalities. Ours is a generation that dearly loves the general. It turns the young loose not on history or government, but on "social studies," not on Mozart or Beethoven, but on "music appreciation," and before the fascinated gaze of the fourteen-year-old it spreads the delights of World History, World

Literature, and World Culture, to be swallowed at one gulp. With Dean Blegen it is the individual experience that counts, and that, in the end, illuminates the experience of the race. He tells us how his own curiosity about Norwegian immigrants "broadened out into a more general inquiry into the interplay of the European heritage and the American environment as creative forces in our national life" and how this led to "the story of immigration as international in setting, with deep roots in the social, cultural, economic, and political life of the modern world." But he never loses sight of the individual as emigrant and immigrant, the individual whose experience is a microcosm of the experience of a large part of the human race.

If we could somehow restore to scholarship these three things — the sense of excitement and of delight, the feeling for the narrative and the dramatic, and the habit of concentrating on the particular and permitting the general to grow out from it — the vexatious problem of attracting the young into those fields of learning that look so forbidding but are in fact so exhilarating would evaporate.

I have been writing about Theodore Blegen as an educator and a scholar whose achievement has been national. But he is more than a national, he is an international, figure. He has addressed himself consistently to one of the most affluent themes of scholarship — the study of the great community of culture, of the transit of civilization from nation to nation and continent to continent. He has written not only of the movement of men and women, but of the migration of ideas and institutions and techniques from the Old World, their modification in the New, and their return once more to the Old World, in unfamiliar and sometimes in explosive form. This, the most neglected area of the study of immigration, is the one that promises most for the future. What Dean Blegen has addressed himself to is a part, small but important, of a large and richly patterned enterprise — nothing less than the restoration of that community of culture which did obtain in much of the eighteenth century and in the United States in the nineteenth as well. Fragmented by the rise of nationalism in the political realm and of romanticism in the intellectual, and then all but shattered by the alliance of political, religious, and racial nationalism in the twentieth century, this community is only now in process of reconstruction. That reconstruction, or restoration, involves the recognition of immigration as a legitimate part not only of our own history, but of the history of the Western peoples, and a recognition of the elementary truth that Dean Blegen has so insistently asserted — that emigrant and immigrant are one. It involves a recognition that the processes of uprooting and transplanting are not only divisive and disintegrating, but in the long run unifying and integrating — one of the methods, indeed, whereby mankind exchanges skills and ideas and whereby it re-creates that sense of unity which is always in danger of being lost. It requires the recognition of the cosmopolitan character of many of the ideas and institutions we are tempted to think of as peculiarly American. It requires, even, the recognition of the potentialities of pluralism in our loyalties — loyalty not alone to a single region or state or nation or people or race, but to the larger community of culture which we all share.

How appropriate then that in honoring Dean Blegen on his retirement from the University of Minnesota a conference should have been designed to explore and interpret this spacious subject to which he has himself contributed so richly.

The conference, held at the University of Minnesota early in 1960, the first of its kind in some thirty years, was in the nature of an animated Festschrift, one in which the hero appeared as an active and lively participant. Most Festschriften are, as all academicians know, miscellaneous affairs; often they seem designed to display the virtuosity of the disciples rather than to celebrate the philosophy of the master. Happily in this case it is the master who is the virtuosi: not only historian and university administrator, writer for the scholar and for the layman, but ballad collector (and singer) and member in good standing of the Baker Street Irregulars. (The bibliography at the end of this volume lists not only Dean Blegen's contributions to immigration literature but some of his writings in other fields — eloquent testimony to the breadth of his interests.) In the circumstances it would have been not only confusing but desperate for Theodore Blegen's colleagues to have tried to reflect all of his interests, and it was the part of discretion as well as wisdom to concentrate on that one which has been most persistent and pervasive.

It is appropriate too that a publication should have come out of that conference, to take its modest place on the shelf beside Theodore Blegen's own writings on immigration. We include in this volume from the conference four substantial papers addressing themselves to new interpretations and four shorter papers designed to explore territory not yet fully charted and surveyed. Rounding out the volume are an essay on immigration as a world phenomenon which it was not possible to give at the conference and one of Dean Blegen's own essays on the literature of immigration which he has permitted us to use here. It is hoped that, just as the miscellaneous ingredients of immigration have themselves assimilated into a rich and colorful if not always harmonious pattern, so the miscellaneous ingredients of this conference will arrange themselves into a scholarly and literary pattern that may both enlist interest and excite the imagination.

HENRY STEELE COMMAGER

Amherst, Massachusetts
January 1961

Table of Contents

IMMIGRATION AND AMERICAN HISTORY

The Study of Immigration

MANY will remember the happy occasion when, with calculated tactlessness, President Franklin D. Roosevelt reminded the Daughters of the American Revolution that they were all the descendants of immigrants. That is, in fact, the quality and the experience all of us have in common; the differences are of degree only in that for some of us the experience is immediate and personal, for others inherited, and for still others vicarious. Immigration is then the oldest theme in our history and the most nearly universal. Yet curiously enough it is one of the last to have enjoyed scholarly consideration. For it was not really until the great immigration of the nineties and the early years of this century that scholars turned their attention to the subject. Even that attention was scholarly only in a relative sense. For the most part it was inspired by considerations of progressivism, of nationalism, or of racism. Of these progressivism was by all odds the most consequential.

Immigration claimed the attention of the progressives because it was so intimately and inextricably associated with those social and economic and moral problems to which they dedicated their energies: slums, and the exploitation of slum-dwellers, sanitation and public health, crime and juvenile delinquency, child labor, the competition of unskilled immigrant labor with organized workingmen, and a host of related issues. It is no wonder that so much of the literature of urban and social reform is also a literature of immigration: Jacob Riis's *How the Other Half Lives*, for example, which aroused the whole country to the shame of the cities, or Jane

[3]

Addams's *Twenty Years at Hull House* which dramatized the failure of the melting pot to melt, or the transparently autobiographical novels of Abraham Cahan and Anzia Yezierska and Shalom Aleichem. Much of the inspiration for the scholarly study of immigration came from such books as these; much, too, came from the massive forty-two volume *Report* of the Immigration Commission of 1910, a report which lent itself to the most diverse interpretations and misinterpretations, and provided ammunition for both informal guerrilla warfare and more formal political battles against the "new" immigration. Out of this ferment came such scholarly works as John R. Commons's *Races and Immigrants in America,* Thomas and Znaniecki's multi-volumed *Polish Peasant in Europe and America,* Mary Coolidge's *Chinese Immigration,* and Edith Abbott's invaluable studies in the historical aspects of immigration.

Nationalism, or pride in the contributions of particular national and racial stocks, found expression in studies often more distinguished by enthusiasm than by scholarly objectivity: thus A. B. Faust's pious but generous *German Element in the United States,* or C. A. Hanna's spirited celebration of *The Scotch-Irish,* or K. C. Babcock's more restrained study of the Scandinavian element, or R. F. Foerster's still valuable book on Italian immigration. The other side of this pride in the contribution of particular immigrant stocks, old and new, was a revival of nativism, but a nativism decked out, now, in the habiliments of scholarship and inspired not by ostentatious racial or religious prejudices, but by respectable sociological and even scientific considerations: thus the writings of scholars like Jeremiah Jenks and E. A. Ross, of social workers like Robert A. Woods, of scientists like Madison Grant and journalists like Henry Cabot Lodge; thus too the immensely popular pseudo-science of Dugdale's *The Jukes* and Goddard's *Kallikak Family.*

These two themes, progressivism and nationalism, largely dominated the first generation of scholarship dealing with immigration. The themes were basically romantic. Progressivists, nationalists, and nativists were all fighting over issues fundamentally moral and sentimental. They set the immigrant apart as a separate and special person, to be welcomed or excluded in accordance with judgments

[4]

about his race, nationality, and historical and sociological experience. They regarded immigration almost entirely from the American point of view. In one way or another almost all of them were involved, consciously or unconsciously, in a great debate: about what the immigrant would do to and for America. Clearly, some immigrants were Good for us, and others were Bad — some were given to industry and thrift, honesty and piety, others to indolence and waste, to vice and crime. So they asked of each potential immigrant: did he cause problems — problems greater than those we should be called upon to bear? Did he assimilate well? Did he cease to be an immigrant and quickly and cheerfully become an American? Would he be a Good Citizen? Did he bring in those bloodstreams, those genes, that are welcome additions to the native stock? This is what most of the scholarly and journalistic writing of that generation was about. Only the novelists — and here and there a gifted publicist — seemed to remember that immigrants were people, too, and that the processes of immigration involved them and their societies as well as America: thus Willa Cather's *My Ántonia*, or Ole Rölvaag's *Giants in the Earth*, or Mary Antin's *Promised Land*.

The next generation — that best represented by three distinguished scholars of Scandinavian descent, George M. Stephenson, Marcus L. Hansen, and Theodore C. Blegen — freed itself to a large degree from these moralistic and romantic preconceptions about immigration, and from nationalist and racist preconceptions as well. We cannot but be struck by the disproportionately prominent role of Scandinavian scholars in this emancipation from the prejudices of the past and ask ourselves whether the relationship is more than fortuitous. After all, not only have three Scandinavians (one, conveniently, from each of the three countries) pioneered in modern immigration studies, but who will deny that of all immigrant novels those from the gifted pens of Ole Rölvaag and Sophus Winther, Johan Bojer and Vilhelm Moberg, have best caught the spirit of the individuals involved. What are the explanations of this interesting situation? Some possible explanations are these: the mainstream of Scandinavian immigration flowed most swiftly in

[5]

the nineteenth century and there has been time for adjustment and perspective; on the whole Scandinavian immigration was drawn from the more respectable elements of society, so it did not excite the animadversions of nativists or, in turn, require the Scandinavians to take refuge in chauvinism; the Scandinavian peoples themselves have a long tradition of cosmopolitanism and have, too, a long tradition of literature and scholarship, and brought these traditions with them to the New World.

This generation, then, managed to rescue immigration studies from exploitation by contending politicians or by chauvinists and racists, and to establish it as a scholarly study. Because their European background was not something they needed to repudiate, and because it was still vivid in their imaginations, they saw immigration as a European — indeed a world-wide — and not merely an American phenomenon, and emphasized the effect of the process on the country of origin as well as upon the country of destination. Because they were thoroughly trained in historical scholarship they addressed themselves assiduously to the collection of facts — the "America letters" for example, official statistics, private papers — and assembled a formidable body of immigration archives. We have thus been able to build scholarly structures on firm foundations. Because they came to maturity in an era when sociology and psychology (not yet called the behavioral sciences, however) were becoming familiar to historians, they interested themselves in the impact of the complex processes of emigration and immigration on the individual and on the societies he left behind and those he helped create. And because that generation repudiated and nullified the artificial distinction between the "old" and the "new" immigration, we have been able to impose unity on the study of a process that embraces not only Europeans, Negroes, Orientals, French-Canadians, and Puerto Ricans, but internal migrations as well.

Theodore Blegen has illuminated all of these areas. His magisterial study of Norwegian immigration began in Norway itself, and lingered on there for an entire volume, thus for almost the first time giving to the country of origin an importance comparable to that customarily conceded the country of ultimate destination; this was particularly arresting for the study of American immigration, for in this country the question has almost always been not where do you come from, but where are you bound. In the two stout volumes which embraced the whole history of Norwegian immigration and in the some forty volumes of publications of the Norwegian-American Historical Association, Blegen provided a substantial body of documentary and statistical material on which later scholars could build. And in the America letters of *Land of Their Choice* and an enchanting collection of ballads and songs, as well as in many essays and translations, he shed light on those social and psychological factors so important to a sympathetic understanding of the complex phenomenon of uprooting, transplanting, and re-creating that is immigration.

The new interests and new points of view stimulated by the generation of scholars typified by Theodore Blegen are amply represented in the papers that follow. Their authors look back, with fresh eyes. And they look forward to new and fruitful explorations.

by OSCAR HANDLIN

Immigration in American Life
A Reappraisal

IN JULY 1921, the *American Journal of Sociology* published a forceful article by Arthur Meier Schlesinger entitled "The Significance of Immigration in American History." The paper was widely read and, no doubt, contributed to the revival of interest in what had theretofore been a relatively neglected field.[1]

The aim of the essay was to set the record straight. It devoted itself to two major themes. In the first place, it pointed to the mixed antecedents of the American population in rebuttal of the argument that the culture of the nation derived from a single overseas source. In the second place it outlined the contributions of immigrants since the colonial period to the material, political, artistic, and idealistic life of the United States.

To the modern reader these points are so familiar as to seem almost commonplace. But they were far from being so in 1921. Four years earlier, under the pressure of wartime emotions, the Congress over President Wilson's veto had enacted a literacy test, the first genuine restriction on immigration in American history. And in 1921, a new law went even farther. It not only set a maximum limit on the number of immigrants who could enter the United States but also established the principle of national quotas

[1] It was rephrased and reprinted in *New Viewpoints in American History* (New York: Macmillan, 1922); *Common Ground*, 1:19ff (1940); and *Paths to the Present* (New York: Macmillan, 1949), pp. 51ff.

[8]

as a means of differentiating among the various types of people who sought entry.[2]

These measures were the culmination of a lengthy, bitter struggle in which a sustained intellectual attack against immigrants was mounted. This attack questioned the utility of immigration to the United States and challenged the capacity of the natives of a large part of Europe to be assimilated into American life.[3]

The Schlesinger essay should thus be seen in terms of the issues of its time. The record had to be set straight in order to eliminate the distortion the restrictionists had introduced into it, and the means of doing so was to prove that immigrants really belonged in the United States by showing the extent of their contributions.

Professor Schlesinger was himself the son of immigrants and was, no doubt, moved to take the position he did by emotional attachments as well as by the intellectual problem itself. In the four decades since then a substantial group of scholarly contributions have added immensely to our knowledge and have helped further to set the record straight. Many of these contributions too were made by immigrants or the sons of immigrants. The names of Marcus L. Hansen, Theodore C. Blegen, and Carl Wittke come immediately to mind. But, however aware these authors were of their own European roots, their products were far removed from the filiopietistic writings of the earlier part of the century. Adhering to rigid codes of scholarship and using scientific methods, these historians did much to create a healthier climate of opinion and to develop an understanding of the place of immigration in American history. Although a great deal still remains to be done, particularly when it comes to the history of such newer immigrant groups as the Poles, the Italians, the Armenians, and the Greeks, the research of the past forty years in this field has made a substantial contribution to American historiography in general.[4]

[2] William S. Bernard, *American Immigration Policy* (New York: Harper, [1950]), pp. 14ff; John Higham, *Strangers in the Land* (New Brunswick, N.J.: Rutgers University Press, 1955), pp. 300ff.

[3] Oscar Handlin, *Race and Nationality in American Life* (Boston: Little, Brown, [1957]), pp. 71ff.

[4] Hansen, *The Atlantic Migration, 1607–1860* (Cambridge, Mass.: Harvard University Press, 1940), and *The Immigrant in American History* (Cambridge,

Those who aspire to treat the subject of immigration in the 1960's, however, must take up the task of that earlier generation in a quite different environment. Both as historian and as citizen the student of today faces new kinds of questions. As a scholar he has been challenged by recent comparative studies and by the development of the social sciences. As a citizen he finds that immigration to the United States is no longer a factor of contemporary importance. But his world is still seriously troubled by the divisive forces of racial and ethnic prejudice and in the East it faces an unprecedented challenge to the American way of life. It is his obligation to apply what knowledge he can assemble to the issues of his own society.

A reappraisal of the role of immigration in American life, therefore, calls not for a restatement or elaboration of the earlier point of view. It demands rather a reassessment and reformulation of the problem in terms that will add meaning to the world of the 1960's and that will draw upon the accumulated knowledge in all the social sciences of the past forty years.

The focus of earlier studies was upon the immigrant as a foreign element injected into American life. They were designed to discover whether the addition of these outsiders to the existing population had beneficial or deleterious effects. Although almost all these works came to a positive conclusion, they approached the immigrant as a newcoming and extraneous addition to indigenous society. Hence in a good many of these works — although not in the best — a concern with the degree to which one group or another was unique, or different from the rest, in its adaptability to American conditions. Hence also that pathetic eagerness to take credit for contributions which produced such futile arguments as those over the nationality of Columbus or the ethnic identity of the Scotch-Irish. Such issues too have lost whatever relevance they ever had.

Mass.: Harvard University Press, 1940); Blegen, *Norwegian Migration to America* (2 vols.; Northfield, Minn.: Norwegian-American Historical Association, 1931, 1940); Wittke, *We Who Built America* (New York: Prentice-Hall, 1939), and *Refugees of Revolution: The German Forty-Eighters in America* (Philadelphia: University of Pennsylvania Press, 1952).

It is, however, also possible to view the process of immigration from within American society. Such a reversal of perspective does not draw so sharp a line between the immigrants and other Americans. It starts rather with the assumption that the entire population of the United States almost from the start was a composite, made up of elements from a multitude of sources. Among these heterogeneous multitudes those who had actually been born in other countries represented only the extreme of a condition that was general to the whole society. The differences between them and the native-born of various sorts, while real, were differences of degree rather than of kind.

Such an approach makes the experience of immigration far more meaningful. By taking the immigrant as a type of American, it also contributes to an understanding of the development of civilization in the United States and sets overseas immigration in a more comprehensive context.

For a long time in American history the movement of peoples across the Atlantic was only one of several types of migration. It was not by coincidence that Frederick Jackson Turner who did so much to call attention to the westward movement also emphasized the importance of immigration. He surmised, although not clearly, that the arrival of millions of newcomers from across the national boundaries was only one aspect of a more general process which also comprehended radical internal shifts of population.[5] Since the international movement was more readily visible than the internal one, the experience of the Irishmen or Italians of the nineteenth century may throw light on the lives of the New Englanders who moved to New York State or Iowa. It may also supply clues to the problems of the "Oakies" who went to California in the 1930's or the southern hillbillies who went to Detroit in the 1940's or the Puerto Ricans and Negroes who arrived in New York in the 1950's.

More generally, insights derived from the extreme experiences of the immigrants have significant implications also for men who

[5] Turner, "Studies of American Immigration," *Chicago Record-Herald*, August–October 1901; Edward N. Saveth, *American Historians and European Immigrants, 1875–1925* (New York: Columbia University Press, 1948), pp. 122ff.

themselves never made a move. For in America even those who stubbornly stayed in the place of their birth often found themselves made aliens by changes in the world about them. Many a Brahmin, grown old on Beacon Hill, looked across the Common in the 1890's and found himself almost as much a stranger to his city as the newcomers who had transformed it. His reactions and theirs were linked; only theirs were more visible.

Among the themes upon which the process of migration throws light is one that has been particularly important in the shaping of modern society. The immigrants experienced in an extreme form what other modern men have felt — the consequences of the breakdown of traditional communal life. This decisive development, about which little is yet known, has significantly influenced American character.[6] One need not feel any sense of nostalgia for the old community to recognize its importance and also the importance of its passing. Whatever judgment one may make upon them, these phenomena are worthy of study. What follows will briefly illustrate the ways in which that breakdown, most clearly to be perceived among the immigrants, influenced significant sectors of American life.

The traditional community embraced a complex of comprehensive, integrated, cohesive, and self-contained institutions. In it people worked out habitual patterns of action and thought. The community was traditional both in the sense that its forms reached back to times out of the minds of living men and also in the sense that it resisted innovations.

The immigrants had destroyed that community in the coming to America. The shock of having done so and the adjustments necessary to compensate were their fundamental social experiences. Persistently but unsuccessfully the immigrants strove to restore their communities. But the disruption was irreparable, with profound effects for American culture in general.[7]

[6] Josiah Royce, *The Hope of the Great Community* (New York: Macmillan, 1916), and *The Philosophy of Loyalty* (New York: Macmillan, 1908).

[7] William I. Thomas and Florian Znaniecki, *Polish Peasant in Europe and America* (Vols. I, II, Chicago: University of Chicago Press, 1918; Vols. III, IV,

Virtually all immigrants made valiant efforts to reconstruct the old communities on the soil of the New World. True, the setting was different; but group after group expressed the longing to perpetuate the forms and to preserve the values which seemed to extend from far back in the past. Even the handfuls of conscious and deliberate rebels who accompanied the larger streams of peasants and artisans were guided by visions formed in the Old World. Only a few men, like Carl Schurz, were sensitive enough to the unfamiliar environment to adjust their sights to the new horizons. The great mass of newcomers could not allow the coming to America to extinguish their heritage. Fear of the possible guilt of having let that happen created a persistent tension among those who strove to preserve the inherited virtues.

The impulse to re-establish the old community was as characteristic of the earliest as of the latest immigrants. In the very first generation of Puritan settlement in New England, the cry was already heard concerning the necessity of preserving the manners and habits of the past.[8] The same appeal was to be pathetically reiterated by the offspring of the Puritans as they advanced into the west. On every frontier, beginning with that on the Connecticut River, and extending in the eighteenth and nineteenth centuries through upper New York State and across Ohio, Indiana, Illinois, on into Iowa, the migrants from New England wistfully urged themselves to preserve that which they were leaving behind. In the architecture and the social order of towns that dot the path of that migration there appear the repeated patterns of the section that was left behind.

George Bates, at the Forefathers' Celebration in San Francisco, thus explained the "New England triumphs on the Pacific." Mentioning the extent of Yankee enterprise in the city, he nevertheless directed his audience to "look upward to the many . . . houses whose pointed spires, rising heavenward, show that they are dedicated to God. The bell summons us to enter, and we do so; and

V, Boston: Badger, 1919–20); Oscar Handlin, *The Uprooted* (Boston: Little, Brown, 1951).

[8] Perry Miller, "Solomon Stoddard," *Harvard Theological Review*, 34:277ff (1941).

there, with suppressed breath, we listen to New England sermons, we join in New England psalms; we look around upon New England wives, New England husbands, New England children." And, the orator added, when "we leave the house of God . . . we enter the school houses of the city. . . . These are New England school houses, New England scholars, New England teachers." Indeed even in the twentieth century the young man who left New England for the great city could find a church supper in New York's Washington Heights identical with that he had known at home.[9]

Historians have rarely perceived the tenacious grip on the inherited culture of the old community. In the 1840's and 1850's, for instance, the clusters of New England settlements across the country formed links in a chain that held together the reform movements of the period. One of the significant aspects of reform in those decades was precisely the effort to preserve the values of the Puritan community under the changing conditions of American society. These agitations often reveal an anxiety about the future and an intention to guard, even if in new forms, the ideals of the past — concerns that also emerge later in the prohibition crusade and account for the intensity with which that issue was debated in the 1920's and 1930's.[10]

So too the negativism and intolerance of the immigration restriction movement and of nativism in general become more comprehensible when viewed in the light of the motives of Americans anxious to prevent their world from changing. Narrow nationalism of this sort was the refuge of men frustrated in the effort to restore the old community. It had numerous counterparts among other American groups; Fenianism and Zionism and a host of similar quests for a homeland embodied the same need for a community to which to belong.[11]

[9] Robert Benchley, "The Typical New Yorker," *20,000 Leagues under the Sea* (New York: Holt, [1928]), p. 228. The quotations are from C. W. Dana, *The Garden of the World, or The Great West* (Boston: Wentworth, 1856), pp. 324ff.

[10] Oscar Handlin, *Al Smith and His America* (Boston: Little, Brown, [1958]), pp. 118ff.

[11] Barbara M. Solomon, *Ancestors and Immigrants: A Changing New England Tradition* (Cambridge, Mass.: Harvard University Press, 1956); Higham, *Strangers*

All that of course was futile. No group could restore the old community or preserve the traditional values against the corrosive forces that transformed these people. Indeed the very process of resistance furthered change.

Yet the struggle was not altogether without results, although not always those anticipated. The most constructive were those in which groups of men turned from the dream of a great all-encompassing community to fill some immediate need in their own lives.

The immigrants in the United States could not restore the community destroyed by migration. But they devised a multitude of organizations to replace it. Mutual assistance, fraternal, religious, and cultural associations supplied them in a fragmentary way with the services the community had performed at home. These organizations have been both more durable and of wider import than is commonly supposed. They have been durable in the sense that they continued to serve a function long after the disappearance of the original immigrating group. They have carried over from the second generation in most groups to play an important role in the lives of the third generation and beyond.[12] Furthermore, such associations have not been confined to peoples conventionally recognized as immigrants through visible differences of language and customs. Analogous organizations developed among the British and also emerged from internal migrations. What was more, the prevalence of this pattern of social action imposed it even on groups not set off by national or sectional differences. It became linked to religious organization and contributed to the ethnic character of American sectarianism.[13]

Such efforts at organization met particular needs but they did not reconstruct the coherent, comprehensive community of the past.

in the Land, pp. 264ff; Oscar Handlin, *Adventure in Freedom: Three Hundred Years of Jewish Life in America* (New York: McGraw-Hill, 1954), pp. 247ff.

[12] Marcus L. Hansen, "The Third Generation in America," *Commentary*, 14:492ff (1952).

[13] From this point of view the histories of the Quakers and of New England societies throughout the country are most illuminating. See also Rowland T. Berthoff, *British Immigrants in Industrial America, 1790–1950* (Cambridge, Mass.: Harvard University Press, 1953), pp. 165ff; William B. Whiteside, *The Boston Y.M.C.A.* (New York: Association Press, 1951), pp. 9ff.

The consequences are reflected to this day in the dominant features of American group life. A society compelled to tolerate a multitude of significant ethnic differences had to develop in a pluralistic fashion, recognizing the right of each group to operate in its own way and yet to suffer in consequence no discrimination or deprivation of the rights of citizenship. Then, too, such a society had to give a wide scope of activity to voluntary as distinguished from governmental organizations. The logical corollary of pluralism in a free society was the abstention by government from interference in spheres in which the points of view of the people it served were not uniform or homogeneous. From the eighteenth century to the present, a continuing adjustment has set the limits within which the state could act and outside of which action could come only through voluntary and fragmented means.

That process had a profound effect upon American institutions, although historians have not yet worked out the details. Bernard Bailyn's study of education in the colonial period reveals clearly and incisively the consequences in one sphere of the disruption of the community caused by migration.[14] Other investigations would show results of comparable significance in philanthropy, in religion, and in the variety of media through which American culture found expression. Much of their history can be written in terms of the collapse of traditional communities, an experience most vividly illustrated in the experience of the immigrants.

A closer view of two primary areas of social activity will reveal some of the ways in which changes in communal life were influential and also the ways in which the development of immigration can illuminate those changes.

The disintegrating influences that grew steadily more important in the eighteenth and nineteenth centuries quickly altered the situation of the family in the community. Observers were quick to notice the disruptive impact of movement upon the families of immigrants, from the Puritans to the Puerto Ricans. What was not so

[14] *Education in the Forming of American Society* (Chapel Hill: University of North Carolina Press, [1960]).

readily evident was that the disorder in such groups was but an acute form of difficulties all Americans encountered.

All the characteristics of strain in the immigrant family had native counterparts. The new conditions that created a difference between the generations and that deprived parents of their educational function, the instability of authority in the absence of communal sanctions, and the constant readjustment in the roles of husband, wife, father, mother, and children have subtly reshaped the family as an institution in the United States. It is not surprising that the subject should have supplied themes for such writers as Mark Twain and Sherwood Anderson.[15] What is surprising is its neglect at the hands of historians.

Some of the tensions that accompanied this transformation have been explored, but rarely with any awareness of the importance of the changing nature of the family. The historians of the women's rights movement, for instance, have generally been content to deal with the demand for equality as if it were simply a product of abstract intellectual propositions. Yet beneath the surface claim to specific legal privileges was a deep emotional unrest generated by the altered position of the woman in the family and by her consequent uncertain status in society.[16]

Other related subjects have not been touched at all. No student of modern society can minimize the importance of changes in the rates of divorce or juvenile delinquency, in family size or attitudes toward birth control and sexuality. Yet general historians have neglected these matters not because the material for an understanding of them is lacking, but because of the difficulty of fitting them into any larger conception of their relationship to society as a whole.

The historians of immigration have been almost alone in dealing with such problems because they had a framework ready-made for doing so. The disorganization of the old extended family in the

[15] The disruption of the family is among the themes of both *Huckleberry Finn* and *Winesburg, Ohio*. See also Sherwood Anderson, *A Story Teller's Story* (New York: Huebsch, 1924), p. 83; Handlin, *Race and Nationality*, Chapter 6.

[16] See, for example, Eleanor Flexner, *Century of Struggle* (Cambridge, Mass.: Harvard University Press, 1959), Chapter 16.

course of migration and the developing individualization of its members were readily described as aspects of the move from the Old World to the New. But these phenomena have also been embedded in the general American experience and can be advantageously explored as consequences of the transformation of the traditional community in the United States.

The breakdown of the community also had important effects upon the relationship of the American to his economy. In the case of the immigrant the shift from one country to another involved a change in occupation that was troublesome enough. But even more troublesome was the fact that the dislocation detached all the modes of earning and spending from their familiar communal settings. The native Americans who migrated across the continent encountered similar difficulties. The hardship of moving from one physiographic region to another or from rural areas to the cities was deepened by the weakness of communal institutions which in turn were further weakened by those very moves.

The consequences were important although they have not yet been historically evaluated. Sons in the United States in the nineteenth century did not often follow the occupations of their parents. The break between the callings of one generation and its successor has been readily related to expanding opportunities, to the ideal of success, and to the utilization of talent to its maximum. But there were also heavy costs in the loss of continuity. Altogether apart from the failures, the hardships, the mistakes, and the wrong decisions that may have been as numerous as the correct ones, the break between the occupational experience of each generation and its successor produced an all-pervasive running tension among Americans.

The economic effects of that tension appeared at every level of American society. It was a concomitant, for instance, of the process by which the market farm took the place of the traditional family farm. The cultivator of the soil in the United States produced not to satisfy his own wants but to sell his crops. As a result he was torn between the incompatible impulses to treat his farm as a home and as a business. On the one hand, he clung to his homestead at any cost. On the other, he concentrated upon staple crops, became involved in commercial speculation, and mechanized and rationalized his modes of production. The resultant difficulties echo through the farmers' grievances from the seventeenth century to the present.

That tension also must be recognized in the problems of labor. We are only at the beginning of our understanding of the phenomena involved in industrialization and urbanization. These processes were not merely economic in character, with the sole issues those of dollars and cents. The experience of the immigrants reveals other more important dimensions.

The immigrant who entered the industrial labor force was not simply oppressed by relatively low wages or by long and difficult conditions of work. Nor, in settling in an urban place, was he troubled only by the physical problems of adjustment. Slums, new habits dictated by life under congested circumstances, the change from living conditions of the countryside that sapped his health — these were all matters of grave concern to him. But they were only part of the story.

To the newcomers life in the cities and labor in the factories seemed to derogate from their qualities as human beings. However harsh their existence had been at home — and often it had been more demanding of their energies than in America — they had been sustained by a community within which they had lived a round of life that was comprehensible in its own terms. All the incidents of the year's labor back there had possessed a meaning and had accorded them a satisfaction, conditioned on no external criteria and validated by the harmony with the world that was their own way from birth to death.

The factory destroyed that. It introduced a new impersonal relationship between employer and employee, subjected the laborer to a routine that took no account of his individuality, and treated him as a piece of machinery less valuable than those of iron because more easily replaced.

More important, the activities of the factory were intrinsically meaningless. Often the laborer had only an approximate impression of the end-product he toiled to produce and rarely did he understand the relationship of his own toiling to it. In time he grasped the central fact of industrialism — that the value of work was not a factor of its productiveness but rather of an inexplicable process that led some men to success and others to failure. By the same token the city was frightening in its anonymity. In it men quickly were overwhelmed by the fear of being lost, for it seemed unrelated to any reality they had earlier known.[17]

The fear, the bewilderment, and the loneliness of the industrial order certainly compounded the difficulties created by low incomes and poor living conditions. These emotional factors undoubtedly shaped the forms taken by efforts to organize labor in the half-century after 1880. The violence and irrational bitterness that then became endemic in American industrial life owed much to the awareness that more was at stake than wages or hours of work. From Homestead to Paterson to Lawrence, the men who resorted to strikes against their employers were aggrieved by the denial of their human dignity.[18]

The difficult adjustment to urban industrial life was not limited to the immigrants or to the lowest sectors of the labor force. The process, most visible among Italian millworkers or Jewish tailors, also touched the experiences of natives of Maine or Ohio or Kentucky. After the depression of 1873, the roads of the nation suddenly seemed thronged with homeless men. For the next four decades the tramp became a characteristic American figure. Estimates of the number of these people at any given time, which range as high as two million, are of course unreliable. But that they were a sizable group seems certain. They merged at times with the armies of migratory workers who took seasonal jobs in agriculture, and in the forests and mines. But some of them also were skilled, like the familiar tramp printer, actor, or promoter who moved from town to town. And these latter figures were, in turn, not far removed from the revivalist, the folk doctor, and the traveling salesman

[17] Oscar Handlin, *Boston's Immigrants* (Cambridge, Mass.: Harvard University Press, 1959), Chapter 3.

[18] See, for example, David Brody, *The Steel Workers* (Cambridge, Mass.: Harvard University Press, 1960).

who occupied the faded rooms of countless modest hotels or rooming houses.[19]

We catch only reflected glimpses of these transients in the observations of more settled people. But these are enough to inform us that the wanderers were men of native birth and antecedents whose restlessness derived from an unwillingness to accept such fixed places as the economy made available to them. Having more opportunity for choice than the foreign-born, they rejected the degradation of factory work and city life and accepted rootlessness as a permanent status.

The cities of mid-nineteenth-century America also contained an enormous population of clerks, bookkeepers, salesmen, foremen, and petty shopkeepers, most of them native-born and almost all of them newcomers from the rural countryside. Their problems of income and housing were not as difficult as those of the unskilled immigrants. But the young men and women who lived in block after block of boarding houses or in monotonous rows of apartments faced social adjustments fully as strenuous as those of the foreigners. The short stories of O. Henry and many of the naturalistic novels of the turn of the century provide documentary evidence of the strains of this process. Such people did not join unions or go out on strike. But their ambitions, frustrations, and grievances received political and social expression, in forms that would be better understood were their sources more clearly recognized.

Among all such groups one can perceive, as among the immigrants, the disruptive effects of the breakdown of the community. In family life and in the economy, the isolation of the individual, the erosion of traditional functions, and the pressure of new conditions form a situation within which many of the characteristic traits of American society were molded.

The consequences for American culture of the breakdown of traditional communities are more subtle, but none the less signifi-

[19] J. J. McCook, "A Tramp Census," *Forum*, 15:753ff (1893); Josiah Flynt [Willard], *Tramping with Tramps* (New York: Century, 1899), Chapters 4–6, and *My Life* (New York: Outing, 1908), pp. 101ff; Melancthon M. Hurd, *System of Commercial Travelling* (Cambridge, Mass.: Riverside Press, 1869), pp. 17ff;

cant. In the disorganization that followed upon migration, controls of every sort grew weaker and leaders found it ever more difficult to shape the desires, attitudes, or tastes of their followers. Furthermore pluralism and voluntarism deprived most groups of any external means of coercion over their members. Individuals who did not wish to conform could break away without fear of any sanctions but those of informal disapproval. Only so long as a tightly knit community life was maintained was effective oversight of the cultural life of the people possible; and that was but rarely achieved except by such millennialist sects as the seventeenth-century Puritans, the Pennsylvania Amish, and the Rappites.

The breakdown was particularly rapid among new immigrants and on the frontier where the lines of communication were most attenuated; and the process was already well advanced in the eighteenth century as the observations of William Byrd revealed.[20]

For somewhat less than a century after the Revolution a good deal of energy went into the effort to develop new and distinctly American forms. Not much then came of the grandiloquent appeals for a national literature or national architecture. But the atmosphere nevertheless encouraged a thriving and genuine folk culture, of which the minstrel show and the circus, the penny press and the lyceum were representative. Inchoate and divided among numerous sectional and ethnic variants, that culture nevertheless responded to authentic popular needs. Within it the immigrants readily found a place.[21]

Indeed it was the immigrant who proved most capable of resisting the later efforts to cram American culture into an artificially defined strait jacket. In the half-century after 1870, the development of American society produced forces that sought to impose an official orderly pattern upon the chaos of folk culture, to define what was good music, good art, good literature, and to exclude from the canons of good taste that which did not fit. The stultifying result, referred

A. D. Crabtre, *Practical Money Making* (Boston: Wilson Brothers, 1885), pp. 218ff, 291.

[20] *Histories of the Dividing Line* (Raleigh: North Carolina Historical Commission, 1929).

[21] See, for example, Carl Bode, *Anatomy of American Popular Culture* (Berkeley: University of California Press, 1959).

to at the time as the genteel tradition, was damaging both to the audience for, and the creators of, art.[22]

The immigrants stood apart. Their separateness enabled them to preserve forms of expression, in the theater, in literature, and in the press, that remained close to their lives. Their culture seemed to outsiders vital and authentic at a moment when a heavy formalism descended elsewhere. After the turn of the century the most creative spirits in the United States were attracted by the immigrants whose "warm, pagan blood" flowed rich by contrast with the austerity about them. Stephen Crane, Theodore Dreiser, Sherwood Anderson, and Hutchins Hapgood, among others, discovered in the urban and rural ethnic enclaves a genuineness of emotions and a reality they could not find elsewhere.[23]

That was why many of them made immigrants of themselves, either by expatriation or by settling in the Bohemias which were the lands of an inner migration. It was not by coincidence that Greenwich Village and Beacon Hill were in close proximity to the immigrant quarters, for here were settled those who deliberately chose the alienation that the immigrant, unwittingly and unwillingly, made part of his situation. And no doubt that association influenced some of the most vital developments of American culture in the twentieth century. In the movies of Charlie Chaplin, in the realistic drama, in the naturalistic novel, and in the music of jazz are refracted impulses of the shattered communities and traditions of which the immigrants were representative.

If it seems paradoxical that in the 1920's many of those who were most eager to rediscover America should have sought to do so by emigrating among the foreign-born, that is of a piece with the other paradoxes with which the history of the United States abounds. Perhaps a nation of immigrants was necessarily too much preoccupied with its own quest for identity and tradition to be aware of the fact

[22] Some aspects of this problem are discussed in Oscar Handlin, *John Dewey's Challenge to Education* (New York: Harper, [1959]), p. 17, and "Comments on Mass and Popular Culture," *Daedalus*, Spring 1960, pp. 325ff.

[23] Anderson, *A Story Teller's Story*, pp. 101, 229; Hutchins Hapgood, *Spirit of the Ghetto* (New York: Funk and Wagnalls, 1902).

that its only identity derived from the diversity of its origins and that its only tradition was that of ceaseless change.

Now that we have arrived at the end of the long process of immigration, some of the elements of a reassessment may have fallen into place.

Such a reassessment would reveal the immense achievements of both the immigrants and the nation as a whole. The story of immigration is a tale of wonderful success, the compounded biography of thousands of humble people who through their own efforts brought themselves across great distances to plant their roots and to thrive in alien soil. Its only parallel is the story of the United States which began in the huddled settlements at the edge of the wilderness and pulled itself upward to immense material and spiritual power.

But the magnitude of the achievement has sometimes blinded observers to the elements of tragedy that were intermixed with it. The history of the United States has been written almost entirely about the smiling aspects of life: rise, progress, growth were the figures of speech that flowed naturally from the pen of the historian. Yet he did less than justice to the drama of the American experience in neglecting its tragic depths.

Certainly tragedy was an intimate part of the life of all immigrants, from those who came to Jamestown to those who only yesterday fled from Hungary. Even those who earned all the exterior measures of success nonetheless carried forever the marks of the losses they suffered from migration.

But this was not the experience of immigrants alone. Nor indeed only of the depressed and underprivileged peoples like the Negroes or Indians. Millions of Americans, native-born and prosperous, lived lives of quiet desperation, the pain of which they compounded by their own inability to recognize its source. But then only a few of their more perceptive contemporaries, and fewer still of the historians, perceived the character of their plight.

It was always tempting, for example, to describe the advance of the frontier as the march of a triumphal army. The frontiersman was a conquering hero, even if he attacked with no banners flying. But this plausible figure of speech concealed a falsification of reality. It glided too readily over the hardships of new settlement, over the debasement of personality and the deterioration of culture that accompanied this process. It left out of account the deserted villages and the abandoned farmhouses. Most important of all it obscured the fact that every man who turned his back upon his home was, in one sense at least, defeated. These restless people were on the move because they could not make out where they were, because old homes and families could no longer contain them. Therein their experience paralleled that of the immigrants.[24]

Indeed, in this perspective such American achievements as the absorption of the immigrants and the settlement of the frontier have the quality of greatness precisely because these were not simply success stories. To recall that these immense accomplishments were rooted in tragic origins, were accompanied by the disruption of traditional communities, and were paid for in heavy human costs is to add the dimension of grandeur to American history.

[24] Walter P. Webb, *The Great Plains* (Boston: Ginn, 1931), pp. 454ff, 505.

by INGRID SEMMINGSEN

Emigration and the Image of America in Europe

ONE of the early Norwegian emigrants tells us, in his reminiscences, that when he and his brother were traveling from place to place in Rogaland — the district from which the very first Norwegian emigrants had come — in the winter of 1836, they heard people talk about a country called America and about an emigrant who had recently paid a visit to his home country, and they saw a letter which had come from America. "This was the first time we heard this name," he says.[1] Three months later the brothers were on their way to America.

This is how the name "America" first appeared in the quiet, conservative, stable, peasant communities of Europe. "Amerika," writes Louis Adamic, who came from a Croatian village, "suddenly, somehow, this name appeared in the village minds. Someone had uttered it. Amerika. But it was still no more than a name." Then a Carniolan trader passed through the village and told of a man from another village who had gone "across the big pond," and who was doing so well in the Michigan copper mines that he allegedly ate meat and white bread every day, and was able to send money home several times a year. Some months later, the first emigrant from Adamic's village left for America. This happened in 1882.[2]

The same thing happened, at different times, in Sweden, Germany, Ireland, Italy, Poland, and many other countries. First the name "America" cropped up, and a short time afterwards the first adventur-

---

[1] *Billed-Magazin* (Madison, Wis.), 1:82–84 (1869).
[2] *From Many Lands* (New York: Harper, 1939), p. 56.

ous, courageous — perhaps maladjusted — individuals departed, and emigration, the nineteenth century's great movement of common people, had achieved contact with new sources among Europe's enormous human reserves. In England internal migrations of considerable proportions preceded mass emigration to overseas countries; in other countries internal migration and emigration arose almost contemporaneously; and in still others emigration virtually broke into hitherto stable conditions. The ferment of emigration pervaded village after village, country after country. Social groups which had lived on the fruits of the earth and by the work of their own hands, which were rooted as firmly in their native soil as were the trees and plants, now broke their traditional ties and journeyed across the ocean. "A man is of all sorts of luggage the most difficult to be transported," Adam Smith had said.[3] Now men moved. They brought change and the idea of change to communities whose essential characteristics had been stability and tradition.

If we were to imagine that those who left for America had been forever cut off from those they left behind, the immediate economic consequences of emigration would have been exactly the same as they in fact were. Any easing in the labor market would have been the same, any loss of manpower and of capital invested in the emigrant would have been the same. But for those of the same social group who remained behind, for friends and relations, the emigrants would, in that case, have been as good as dead. If no communication could have been established, the emigrants would, after some time, have been forgotten, or fantastic legends about them might have arisen, legendary tales with no foundation in reality.

But the emigrants to America wrote home. They sent letters and, later, newspapers, photographs, and maps; they sent money and tickets. A few returned home and could personally tell those who had remained behind about the new country. In some countries, many returned home toward the end of the nineteenth century, and they remained in the old country.

The private letter has a long history. Before the time when it was written on paper, it had been written on clay tablets, on papyrus,

[3] *Wealth of Nations* (Edinburgh: A. and C. Black and W. Tait, 1845), p. 34.

and on parchment. But in the lives of the farmers, artisans, and work-men of most European countries it was a novelty. The private letter, as a means of contact for the common people, followed in the wake of emigration. Postal services were also of long standing, but they had not been designed to fill the need of these social groups for private communication. We may, in fact, say that it was Rowland Hill's successful campaign for penny postage in Britain which eventu-ally made it economically possible for the lower classes to avail them-selves of the postal services and to send and receive news by means of letters.

Now the letter made its appearance in the daily round of farmers and workmen; often, perhaps most often, the letter from America. At first it was a rarity, a strange event which caused a stir far beyond the recipient's immediate circle. Later, as the flow of emigration in-creased, more and more letters arrived. The sensation caused by the first letters may have died down gradually, but a letter from America was never looked upon as a common, everyday event. We know that it was opened with great excitement and perused with in-terest. It was read by many people, its contents were told and retold, and discussed. Often it was copied and sent on to others — we know that this happened in Norway — and some of the letters were even published in newspapers. In Norway such publication caused lively discussion of emigration and of American conditions. In 1862, a Norwegian farmer wrote to his children and grandchildren in Amer-ica: "On Easter Monday, over by the church, Ingeborg was told that a letter had come for us from America, and we went to fetch it immediately and read it with great excitement." "Don't write about everything in *one* letter," another Norwegian asked his friend in America, "you know how it is — someone wants to read your letter, another wants to borrow it, and there are some things, after all, which do not concern everybody. . . ." Or, as has been said about the "Amerikay letther" in Ireland: it was "borne in in triumph and opened with joy."[4]

[4] Ingrid Semmingsen, *Veien mot Vest* [The Way West], Vol. II (Oslo: Aschehoug, 1950), p. 270; Arnold Schrier, *Ireland and the American Emigration, 1850–1900* (Minneapolis: University of Minnesota Press, 1959), p. 40.

Many emigrants were themselves able to write, though their orthography and grammar might be faulty; others had to seek help. A Norwegian pioneer wife in Iowa said that she always had to help her neighbors to write letters. The illiterate Italian newcomer to the United States went to his *paesano,* who acted as banker and lawyer, found employment for him, supplied him with paper and stamps, and wrote his letters. On the other side of the Atlantic, in the streets of Naples, one could see a replica of the ancient Roman scribe: the public letter-writer. These scribes were busy with American correspondence — Italians writing by dictation to their friends in the United States.[5]

Some such letters from America had been coming to Europe for a long time. In England, letters from New England had been "venerated as a Sacred Script,"[6] and intellectual circles in Europe had been vividly interested in America and in "the American experiment" from the time of the War of Independence. This interest remained alive — the great number of travelogues and descriptive accounts about America which were published in Europe bear witness to this. But the mass emigration of the nineteenth century brought with it something new: social groups which had lived largely without impulses from the outside world, which had been more or less self-contained within their own narrow community, were now, through their own members, brought into close touch with a hitherto unknown and different society. For this reason, we are not concerned here with the picture of America sketched by the travelers in their books, nor with that which the educated public gained from newspapers or other sources, but with that picture of America which mass emigration created for those in the social classes from which the emigrants were recruited, and with the influence which this impression of a new and unknown world and this contact with it had on those who remained behind in the old country. We may safely

[5] Pauline Farseth and Theodore C. Blegen, trans. and eds., *Frontier Mother: The Letters of Gro Svendsen* (Northfield, Minn.: Norwegian-American Historical Association, 1950), p. 125; Robert F. Foerster, *The Italian Emigration of Our Times,* Harvard Economic Studies, no. 20 (Cambridge, Mass.: Harvard University Press, 1919), pp. 391–92; F. L. Dingley, *European Emigration* (Washington, D.C., 1890), p. 221.

[6] Theodore C. Blegen, *Land of Their Choice: The Immigrants Write Home* (Minneapolis: University of Minnesota Press, 1955), p. 4.

say that this form of direct contact and influence no longer exists. It belonged to the period of mass emigration, it was brought about by those who had known the old and experienced the new. Only these people knew both worlds, and only they could know — or feel — what news would interest those at home, what they would understand, and how the news should be worded.

It would be wrong to say that these "agricultural communities" in the various European countries — even those untouched by industrialism — had lived through the centuries in complete isolation. Various cultural impulses had penetrated; the folk music, folk dancing, and folk art of the countries of Europe show clear signs of this. But these impulses had filtered through to the farmers by way of the higher classes within their own country, and the process had been slow. They had been digested and changed, they had been adapted to the old social pattern and had become a part of it. With the letter from America came news of recent happenings to one from their own ranks now in a new environment.

Some of the emigrants wrote about the soil, domestic animals, and houses in a settlement in the Middle West, others about the working conditions a maid in an American family might expect, yet others about wages and working conditions in the mines of Michigan or about life in a New York tenement. But they all had this in common: their letters described — and often praised — the new, the unknown. Thus, in the words of Theodore C. Blegen, "the nineteenth century witnessed a new discovery of America. It came about, not through the daring of a new Columbus, but as a consequence of letters written by immigrants to the people of the Old World. It was a progressive and widening discovery. . . ."[7]

The common factor for all those who remained behind in the Old World, regardless of the European country in which they lived, was the contact with the unknown, foreign country, the communication of impulses by way of letters and by personal associations. Now the main stress lay on the one, now on the other, varying from time to time, from place to place. If we ask what impulses were communicated, what were the main features of the picture of America which

[7] *Ibid.*, p. 3.

those at home were gradually able to build up in their minds, what significance did this contact and these impulses have for them — then it becomes more difficult to give a precise or exhaustive answer, partly because the different regions of America are different in character, partly because America underwent considerable change in the course of the nineteenth century, and partly because the recipients lived under such different conditions in the various European countries. Consider, for example, the difference between Great Britain, whose relations with America were centuries old, and isolated communities on the fiords of Norway, or villages in Poland. Another fact which makes it difficult for us to provide an answer is that impulses from without are assimilated by and within the human mind; such assimilation cannot be catalogued and only rarely leaves traces on documents. Finally, we have the practical difficulty, expressed thus by Professors Curti and Birr: "Despite the considerable evidence regarding the impact of the returned immigrant, the subject has barely been scratched."[8] This study must, therefore, be based on the Norwegian material with which I am acquainted. I can no more than dip into the material from other countries occasionally, in order to throw light on some of the general problems I shall discuss.

European historical research has paid little attention to the influences of emigrations on the Old World — just as only scant attention has been devoted to the study of the emigration movement itself. The movement is so important, and seems to have had such far-reaching consequences, that one would think it deserving of greater interest. Perhaps there is a psychological explanation: the politically and socially influential groups in the various European countries felt bitter toward those who had shown their dissatisfaction with their motherland by emigrating, and historians who shared this attitude have shrunk from studying the emigration movement and its impact. Today, when emigration as it unfolded itself in the nineteenth century has become truly a thing of the past and can be

[8] Merle E. Curti and Kendall Birr, "The Immigrant and the American Image in Europe, 1860–1914," *Mississippi Valley Historical Review*, 37: 203–30 (September 1950).

regarded with greater detachment, the study of its history is gaining in interest in Europe.

American scholars, on the other hand, have for some time been concerned not only with the significance of immigration for American society, but also with the impact of the contact with America on Europe. The first work in this field was done by two scholars at the University of Minnesota: Theodore C. Blegen and George M. Stephenson, both of whom collected letters written home by American immigrants. At the Congress of Historical Sciences in Oslo in 1928, Professor Blegen appealed for international cooperation in the collection and preservation of "America letters" and related material. "Such historical cooperation," he said, "if extended, might lead to the discovery and preservation, in many European countries, of new materials of value for an understanding of that vast modern migration which furnishes in its myriad ramifications one of the great themes of American history and which reminds one again of the racial and cultural bonds between the new world and the old." [9] It is a pity that this international cooperation has not yet been realized.

Meanwhile, other American scholars have studied this subject, and a great deal of their attention has been directed toward the Scandinavian countries. In 1934, Brynjolf J. Hovde wrote an article about the effects of emigration upon Scandinavia, and he touched upon this theme, too, in his work *The Scandinavian Countries*. In 1946, Franklin D. Scott, in a more general discussion of the American influences in Norway and Sweden, laid particular stress on the impulses transmitted through contact between the emigrants and their friends and relations in the old country. [10] Professors Curti and Birr, in their article "The Immigrant and the American Image in Europe, 1860–1914," also gave much attention to the Scandinavian countries.

Is all this presumptive evidence that the effect of America letters and other contacts with emigrants was particularly consequential in the Scandinavian countries? If so, can it be due to strong appeals from the immigrants in the new country, or to ardent receptiveness

[9] *The America Letters* (Oslo: Norwegian Academy of Science, 1928), p. 24.

[10] Hovde, "Notes on the Effects of Emigration upon Scandinavia," *Journal of Modern History*, 6:253–79 (September 1934); Scott, "American Influences in Norway and Sweden," *Journal of Modern History*, 18:37–47 (March 1946).

in those who stayed home? Or is this Scandinavian emphasis mere chance, or a reflection of the fact that the source material in these countries is limited and easily handled?

The America letters to Norway came to a country with a social hierarchy more flexible than most other European countries had. There was, for instance, no nobility, and under the Constitution of 1814 — the most liberal in Europe — all farmers owning or leasing registered land were entitled to vote. In the 1830's — the Jacksonian Era in American history — the farmers gradually began to make use of the political power invested in them by the Constitution; and in the national assembly an agrarian group made its appearance in opposition to the public and government officials, theretofore the most influential class in the country, socially and politically.

Norway as a society remained predominantly rural for a long time; industrialization started slowly in the 1840's, and made more rapid progress after 1850. With the disruption of the old, self-contained rural society and the opening up of new economic and social possibilities, this industrial development brought in its wake fundamental, far-reaching social changes. New political demands were heard, such as those for an extension of the franchise to include new social groups, for parliamentarianism, and for trial by jury. A new feature of the life of the community was the appearance of private voluntary organizations, of important popular movements such as the temperance, religious, and youth movements, the consumer cooperatives, political associations, and the people's high schools which gave the rural youth not only instruction but also a new outlook on life. Rural youth indeed were beginning to break with old traditions in all aspects of life and were filled with new social ambition and drive. As agriculture in its transition from a self-contained to a money economy experienced a sharp depression, young people found social and economic opportunities in the new industries, in public works, in education, or through emigration to America. They wanted to come out into the world, they wanted to become something different from what their fathers had been.[11]

[11] For works in English on Norwegian history of this period see Brynjolf J. Hovde, *The Scandinavian Countries, 1720–1865: The Rise of the Middle Classes*

Into this Norwegian society, where internal social change, internal migration, and emigration began simultaneously and side by side, and were parts of one and the same development, poured an endless stream of America letters. They came to the homes of hard-working, independent small farmers and to the poor crofters' cots, to men and women in the vigor of middle life and to youth looking to the future.

Some of them told of disillusion and disappointment and, especially in the earlier years, of mistakes in locating land, of sickness and death; but the majority revealed a positive response to and an acceptance of American conditions. They told of fertile land bought at a low price, land that was level ground and easy to cultivate. In Norway a man would have to work his whole life to bring ten or fifteen acres under the plow, but the emigrants in America boasted of cultivating that many acres in a couple of years. The letters told of higher wages and richer opportunities in the New World, but cautioned that all of this called for hard work. It was these reports of the richer economic opportunities and especially of inexpensive land that undoubtedly weighed most heavily in the scale for those who had emigration in mind.

Not all the letter-writers confined themselves to descriptions of their personal life — the number of cattle they owned or the barn they had built. Often they tried to give a more general description of American social and political conditions, to interpret America to their friends and relatives in the old country. And for a long time (up to the last decade of the nineteenth century) they generally praised what they found in the New World. In these years the skeptical notes came mostly from that minority who, for lack of money or for other reasons, did not manage to join the prairie communities but were forced instead into unskilled work.

The rural Norwegian emigrant seemed to adjust himself with relative ease to the pioneer conditions of the Middle West. He was accustomed to toil and struggle against the forces of nature, while

(Boston: Chapman and Grimes, 1943), Vols. I–II; Karen Larsen, *A History of Norway* (Princeton, N.J.: Princeton University Press, 1948); Peter A. Munch, *A Study of Cultural Change* (Oslo: Aschehoug, 1956); Ingrid Semmingsen, "The Dissolution of Estate Society in Norway," *Scandinavian Economic Review*, 2:166–203 (1954).

local self-government and egalitarian democracy conformed to the patterns of culture and aspirations he brought with him from home. He could to a certain extent build on his own foundations; and after a while he could understand and interpret. Despite all tendencies to clannishness, to living apart in Norwegian-American communities, he took part in the building of a new society where none had existed before. This was the positive side of that pioneer experience which included so much of struggle and drudgery in everyday life. He liked his new life, and when he spoke, it was as an ardent exponent of that midwestern society which was his America. In the words of George M. Stephenson the Scandinavian emigrant became "an evangelist preaching the gospel to the heavy-laden." [12]

We find many characteristic expressions of this spirit in the history of Norwegian immigration. There is, for example, the so-called Muskego Manifesto of 1845, in which eighty Norwegian settlers answered the reports which had been published by the Norwegian press on America, emigration, and the conditions of life in the New World. "We have no expectation of gaining riches," they wrote to the folks back home, "but we live under a liberal government in a fruitful land, where freedom and equality are the rule in religious as in civil matters, and where each of us is at liberty to earn his living practically as he chooses. Such opportunities are more to be desired than riches. . . ." [13]

We find this spirit again in another collective enterprise, "The Chicago Correspondence Society" of 1848, organized specifically to correct "erroneous impressions" of America in Norway. One of its letters reads: "Here it is not asked, what or who was your father, but the question is, what are you? . . . Freedom is here an element which is drawn in, as it were, with mother milk, and seems as essential to every citizen of the United States as the air he breathes. It is part of his life. . . . It is a national attribute, common to all. Herein lies the secret of the equality seen everywhere. . . ." [14]

[12] "When America Was the Land of Canaan," *Minnesota History*, 10:246 (September 1929). See also Peter A. Munch, "Social Adjustment among Wisconsin Norwegians," *American Sociological Review*, 14:780–87 (December 1949).

[13] Blegen, *Land of Their Choice*, pp. 193–94.

[14] *Ibid.*, p. 203.

Once this pattern was established, it was perpetuated and brought to the newcomer. Upon his arrival he might be told by an older Norwegian immigrant: "You see, here we don't even have to take our cap off for the vicar. That is some difference from the old country!" And the newcomer would at once have an example of American social equality for his first letter home.

The contents of the letters were easily understood by the recipients at home. What they told of land and wages augmented the flow of emigration; what they told of hardships and sickness was to the recipients so much in the nature of life that it was not frightening; and what they told of social and political conditions conveyed a picture of a land where local self-government and democracy were carried to a greater perfection than at home and a society based on the principle of social equality, where the common man and honest work commanded greater respect than at home.

For those at home in the old country, these reports were not merely fantastic tales from a strange, unreal dream world: the letters gave form to thoughts that seemed familiar and natural to those who read them; they touched upon themes that were deeply interesting to farmers and workmen everywhere in the land. Of course there was a difference between Norway and America, a great difference — both the writers and the recipients discovered that; but even so, the difference was not so great as to make comparison impossible. The example from America was full of interest and of meaning; those who read the America letters could believe that, if they but exerted themselves, they too could achieve such conditions here at home, that the impulses from without could be applied to the home front. The letters therefore came to be a stimulus, not the stuff of a daydream. What Einar Haugen says about Norwegian emigrants is also applicable to those who stayed at home: "But the men of the nineteenth century were like Adam and Eve after they had tasted the apple of knowledge: they suddenly discovered that they were hungry. The apple they ate was the news of America which came to them through their newly-founded newspapers, their improved school systems, their previously migrated relatives, the letters and books about America. They emigrated because they had learned to be dissatisfied, and because a changing world had provided them with a hope of escape from their dissatisfaction."[15]

This wish to escape or to change conditions which seemed increasingly undesirable existed at home too. So the news in the America letters stimulated a lively interest in politics, in popular movements and social questions — it was the "apple of knowledge" for Norwegian society. The knowledge of relatives who were doing well in America increased the individual's self-confidence; it was delightful to see an emigrant back in Norway talk to the vicar as his equal; it was a comfort to know that, if his hopes were not fulfilled in Norway, he too could emigrate to America.

All this appears perhaps most clearly from the use which the farmer-politician Sören Jaabaek made of the reports about America. Jaabaek, a strange cross between a conservative and a radical liberal, was the first to organize the rural voters into associations; and in the 1860's, these gained tremendous support. Jaabaek was in constant and direct touch with the electors, to a far greater extent than any other politician. From 1865 to 1879 he published a newspaper, *Folketidende* (Newspaper for the People), which soon reached the considerable circulation of 17,000, mostly among farmers. It is a proof of America's high reputation among the common people, and of the relevancy of the reports from America to political discussion at home, that Jaabaek saw fit to fill his paper with information about America. In the period 1865–73, hardly an issue appeared without a mention of America in some connection or other and a comparison of American conditions with those in Norway. Jaabaek expressed it thus: "My readers have noticed that I think very highly of the constitution of the United States . . . I regard my reports about America as being part of my policy."[16] Whether the subject under discussion was conscription, freedom to choose one's own employment, popular education, or, most frequently, public officials and their position in society — whatever the subject, Jaabaek illustrated his arguments with examples taken from American political or social life. He

[15] *The Norwegian Language in America: A Study in Bilingual Behavior* (2 vols.; Philadelphia: University of Pennsylvania Press, 1953), I, 22.

[16] *Folketidende*, January 25, 1871.

would certainly not have used America so systematically as an example if he had not thought it one which would appeal to his readers and would be useful to his own policy, and if he had not known that the rural voters knew and admired America and that a comparison of America and Norway would be likely to stimulate them to political activity.

At the beginning of the 1880's Norway experienced a severe constitutional crisis, caused by conflict over the establishment of parliamentarianism; with this, a new form of contact between the emigrants and the Liberal opposition party in Norway came into being. Norwegian-Americans formed Liberal associations. All Norwegians in Minnesota's Twin Cities were at that time "Liberals with a vengeance," so we were informed; they held mass meetings, sent addresses to the leader of the opposition, Johan Sverdrup, and collected money. Originally, the idea was that this money should be used to purchase rifles for a national, voluntary organization of rifle clubs, supported by the adherents of the Liberal party; but this met with doubts and reluctance both in Norway — where it went against the constitutional ideology of the Liberal party — and among the emigrants. The money was eventually used as a fund to further Liberal politics.

The crisis in Norway was brought to an end in the summer of 1884 with the leader of the opposition forming the first Norwegian government based on a parliamentary majority. Thus the topical purpose of the Liberal associations in America disappeared, and they soon faded away or were dissolved. They did not have any significant effect on the constitutional conflict in Norway and the support they gave to the opposition was of minor importance. Yet one of the many factors behind the strong political passion that consumed Norwegians during these years was the impact of the America letters. Sverdrup said this in his own distinctive rhetorical style in an address to the association Fram in Minneapolis in 1883: "There are two matters which the people of Norway will not forget: the debt of gratitude which all the free nations of Europe owe to the great republic in the West, which was the first to raise the star-spangled banner of liberty and equality; and the powerful influence exerted by Norwegian emigrants who have become citizens of the United States and by their sons, through thousands and thousands of exchanges of thoughts and ideas with their friends and kin here in the old country — an influence which has roused the people of Norway to activity and has opened their eyes to the blessings of liberty."[17] Let us advance the following hypothesis: the fact that 69,000 Norwegians — more than 20 per cent of the electorate of a country with strong monarchical traditions — voted for a republican form of government in 1905 may have been largely due to the prestige of America, created in part by the America letters.

Many religious revivals and dissenting movements in both Norway and Sweden were also influenced from America. Dr. Stephenson has shown this in his *Religious Aspects of Swedish Immigration*, and Gunnar Westin of Uppsala has worked on the same subject. Methodism was brought to Norway by an emigrant sailor who for many years worked as a missionary for the Norwegian-American Methodist Church; and from the point of view of organization, the Norwegian Methodist Church was, during the entire nineteenth century, a subdivision of the Norwegian-American Methodist Church, with many of the Norwegian Methodist preachers receiving their training in America. Swedish-Americans brought the Baptist church to Sweden, whence it came to Norway. The temperance movement too received impulses from America, though these did not always come by way of the Norwegian-American milieu but were rather the result of the prestige America had attained through emigration. But other popular movements, such as the consumer cooperatives, had few or no ideological models in America.

These Norwegian associations and popular movements, religious and secular, often joined forces in demands for political reforms. They themselves were democratic in structure, their boards and officials elected by the vote of the members. They were practical schools of democracy and their leaders were often inspired by American ideas, mostly absorbed through contact with America. The letters from America brought knowledge, created an interest in society beyond narrow, local confines, and, in the intensely patriotic climate of Norway in the second half of the nineteenth century, stimulated

[17] *Dagbladet*, October 26, 1883.

activity. Through them the common man was given new arguments in his struggle for social and political justice.

In Norway there is some evidence that contemporary opinion was well aware of the influence exerted by the America letters on the old country. The Liberal newspaper *Dagbladet* wrote that the letters from America and the knowledge of America's free institutions imparted by them had been just as important as the work of the political organizations in exciting the great interest in politics shown by the farmers in the 1868 election. "During his daily work, perhaps when something goes wrong, it is natural that the farmer's thoughts turn to that country where some of his family live, most often doing well; and by comparing conditions over there with those at home he discovers that a good deal could have been different and better in this country, too. He is no longer mentally confined by the mountains and fiords surrounding him. His horizon has been widened, and he is receptive to impressions which change much in the old, traditional way of thinking, and which arouse him to a realization of his position in society." One newspaper contributor called America "the mental locomotive of the whole world," while another thought that the impact of "vigorous America" was like "sparks of fire, or rather, electric sparks." The reports from America "arouse strange longings in the farmers and crofters of our poor mountain valleys, weighed down, as they are, by hard work and worries about their livelihood," wrote a third. "Yes, I myself have seen how the news of a poor brother becoming wealthy and attaining an independent position after a few years in America has brought new light to dim, dejected eyes."[18]

Eilert Sundt, regarded as the founder of Norwegian social anthropology, knew more about the rural communities of Norway than anyone else in his time. In 1873, he called the letters from America one of the age's new "means of power" and placed them in the same class with agricultural schools, people's high schools, the new rural political organizations, new religious organizations, and the newspapers, which were beginning to be read by the farmers and common people.

Alexander Kielland, of all the novelists of the golden age of Nor-

[18] Semmingsen, *Veien mot Vest*, II, 475.

wegian literature the most acute observer of society and its sharpest critic, lets one of his characters say that the Norwegian upper classes have almost been at a standstill for a couple of generations and that every new idea with which they are confronted fills them with fear and apprehension. The attitude of the common man, however, is different — and better:

Firstly, they do not read the newspapers of the pillars of society, where the whole world is turned upside down *in usum delphini.* Dead ideas embellished with fresh invective: concealment of the real face of the times, and the daily repetition of the primeval truths such as that America is the home of the blackguards, France that of the *communards,* Kristiania the home of wisdom, Stockholm that of virtue! They do not read that. . . . But what they do read is something most of us never think about — they read and re-read the thousands of letters which year after year pour in from the Norwegians in America. And these, you see, are a better source of education than any newspapers or books. For through them, *the people for the first time learn from those of their own milieu,* in their own language, their own way of thinking — and no one can fully understand a way of thinking alien to him. Think of all the criticism of the conditions here at home, in all spheres, which these letters contain — straightforward, easily understood verdicts and comparisons coming from a cousin or from good old Uncle Lars who is so trustworthy and knows such a lot about everything.[19]

Printed communications were also sometimes sent to and fro between the emigrants and their relatives in the home country. The Norwegian-American press, as Kenneth Bjork has noted, was a forum for discussion and the exchange of news from the various settlements in America and the home parish or district in Norway. Every issue of *Skandinaven* and *Decorah Posten* brought letters from Minnesota and Dakota, from Gudbrandsdal or Telemark.[20]

Unfortunately, we have no statistics for the circulation of Norwegian-American newspapers in Norway in the nineteenth century. *Decorah Posten* still sent as many as 3,000 copies to Norway in the 1940's, and old people in Norway remember that in their youth

[19] *Fortuna* (Oslo: Gyldendal, 1941), pp. 366–67.
[20] *West of the Great Divide: Norwegian Migration to the Pacific Coast, 1847–1893* (Northfield: Norwegian-American Historical Association, 1958), p. 11.

Decorah Posten, Skandinaven, Visergutten, and others were found in many homes. They were never as numerous as the private letters, but they came regularly and they were read by neighbors and friends in addition to the subscriber himself. They, too, spread knowledge about America, made America a neighbor, a country quite different in their view from any other foreign lands because near relatives lived there.[21]

Impulses from America were also transmitted by those emigrants who returned to the old country, whether for a visit or for good. The first to return from America — and most of these were only visiting the old country — created a sensation. People walked for miles to see them, to make sure they were real — to talk to them, to hear about this new country on the other side of the ocean. From a valley in western Norway comes this account of the impression made by visiting Norwegian-Americans in the 1850's. Charles Loring Brace tells of his visit to Vossevangen — "one of the more retired valleys of Norway":

By a singular chance there were two other persons from America in our inn — two Norwegians who had been some fifteen or sixteen years in our Western country, had made their fortunes, and were returned, partly for a visit, and perhaps partly for a speculation — to bring profitable immigration to their own "claims," or town-lots. They were said to have left the village poor boys, and now they came back as grandees. Through all Sunday there was a levee of their friends in their room, smoking, drinking coffee, and occasionally a

[21] It would be interesting to know to what extent the newspapers of the various immigrant groups were sent to their respective old countries, and to analyze their contents. In England regular American newspapers had a wide circulation. As J. M. Ludlow, the publicist, wrote in an article in 1894: "The pouring forth, during many years, of emigrants into the United States had produced a reflex action which began, probably, with the sending over of copies of American newspapers — often in place of a letter — from emigrants to their families in the old country. This grew into the subscribing regularly for such papers, and to the establishment of offices for their sale. In the autumn of 1851, I travelled, mostly on foot, through a large portion of the manufacturing districts of Lancashire and Yorkshire, mixing chiefly with working-men, and in many cases was received at their homes. I was amazed at the large diffusion of American newspapers. I was told that in the factory districts there were nearly as many American papers as English sold to working-men; that there was scarcely an operative's home where at least a copy of one was not to be found." ("The Growth of American Influence over England," *Atlantic Monthly,* 74:619–20 (November 1894).)

bottle of wine. The contrast between the Americanized Norwegians and their countrymen was instructive. These two were complete Westerners of the middle class — "Hail-fellow" with every one, sharp, alert, self-asserting, almost nervous in busy activity, with swarthy faces, blue coats, and gorgeous velvet waistcoats, and very expensive dress and outfit — using the worst American drawl, and smoking and chewing incessantly. Their friends and companions from whom they came, were stately, moderate people, dressed in national jackets and breeches, or coats trailing to the feet, with blonde faces and long light hair parted in the middle. The women in red bodices, and with brilliant head-tire. They moved, one after another, with slow dignified pace to the inn and in the room they seemed like judges or princes before these restless popinjays of men. Their faces had an austere, impenetrable cast as they watched the vulgar activity or listened to the loud stories of the American Eden. There was a wonderful revelation of contrasts. Only once the national reserve broke down, and their pride in their successful countrymen burst forth — when they heard the Norwegians talking English with us they laughed in exultation, and crowded near. I found my two countrymen very good fellows. They said their journey was costing them frightfully as every one imagined an American must have his pockets lined with gold, and they objected to no bills. We had often encountered the same impression about ourselves, and pretty effectually corrected it for future American travellers.

They found Norway horribly dull — everything so much behind-hand — farming fifty years behind the age. They were homesick already. Yet this valley they thought one of the finest districts in the whole country . . . but the people were slow. They *would not* attempt any improvement.

Then they could not stand this dress of the women — waists way up under the arm, and short petticoats! They had been to the church that morning, for the sake of old times, but this absolution by the priest was too much for them. "It is behind the age, Sir!"

I said I liked the service, and the earnest, devout appearance of the people. "Oh, yes: but that humbug of a minister! He won't come near us, because he thinks we are carrying off his people to America! Old Norway don't do beside the West, Sir! Take a cigar? — We'd show 'em a thing or two if they'd come out to Wisconsing! Git back to Elecksion, sir?" "Yes. How do you vote?" "FOR FREMONT — to be sure, sir!" [22]

[22] *The Norse Folk, or A Visit to the Homes of Norway and Sweden* (London: R. Bentley, 1857), pp. 97–99.

Some days later, Charles Loring Brace encountered another returned emigrant who talked in the same way as the two at Voss:

"I cannot bear it here, sir," said he, "in no way. I had a kind o' expected to have stayed till fall — but it's too lonesome. There isn't nothing going on." "I suppose you are very well off now in America," said I. "Oh yes; I have one of these farms of mine own in Wisconsin, and I let it out for the summer. When I was here, I used to have a terribly hard time. I tell you, sir, I've worked from four o'clock till eight, month in and month out, and only got seven cents a day and found! They say now it's about sixteen cents." I asked about machines. "They don't know nothing about machine work. Look at 'em — there they'd keep six men for a week to mow twelve acres, and I'd just take one of our mowing-machines and dew it all in one day. They never seed a reaper, nor even a horse-rake, nor any of 'em!"[23]

The immediate effect of these early references was, however, more to augment the stream of emigration than to stimulate activity at home. The early Norwegian emigrants went to America in order to remain there, and this fact did not lessen the impact of emigration on Norway, or the contact between the two countries. We might even venture the paradox that the impulse from America was stronger the more permanent the settling there, and that the letter was a more refined form of communication, exercising a stronger influence, than the oral narrative of the returned emigrant. Once written, the words of the letter stood; the personal account might be changed.

In the late 1880's, however, a new type of emigration from Norway developed. From the coastal districts, especially of southern Norway, from districts with seafaring traditions of old standing, people went to America for some years in order to earn and save money for the purpose of investing it at home. The census of 1920 showed that, in the county of Vest-Agder, one in four of the men over the age of fifteen had been in America. It also showed that 72 per cent of those returned from America had spent from two to nine years there, while one fifth had been there longer. The majority had returned home while they were still fairly young — over 40 per cent before they reached the age of forty. The census also showed that, for the majority of them, their stay in America resulted in a certain social

[23] *Ibid.*, p. 127.

advancement. We may reasonably believe that those who were most successful in America and adapted themselves with comparative ease stayed there. On the other hand, those who returned were not, generally, the failures. On returning home, many of these temporary emigrants became farmers, or they again took over the farms looked after by their families during their absence. Among the returned Norwegian-Americans over the age of sixty-five, there were comparatively few requiring public assistance — fewer than among their contemporaries who had not been in America, and a far greater number of them lived on their savings.[24]

These returned emigrants most often invested their savings in agriculture and, from the 1880's and 1890's onwards, also in fishing. The medical officers of health in the coastal districts often mention them in the annual reports submitted to the public health authorities. The medical officers were very interested in hygiene — the field of bacteriology was rapidly expanding — and they noted time and again that those returning brought with them new impulses affecting hygiene. They also mention that those who had been in America showed more daring than the stayers-at-home in trying new agricultural methods. They were among the first to acquire agricultural machinery; they tackled extensive clearing schemes. The medical officers were agreed that the money they brought home was important enough (this was turned into better dwellings and better outbuildings) but what was still more important was that they, during their stay in America, had learned to work rationally, to use their time to the best advantage. To quote one of these medical officers, they had "acquired a wider outlook," they were not bound by "the narrow and meagre conditions at home."

Sometimes the returned emigrants attempted enterprises which were bound to fail, as when some tried to grow tobacco in the county of Sogn in the west of Norway, but even in this case the district medical officer noted the good influence they exercised on their neighbors in showing them that every job must "be done with care, hard work and perseverance."[25]

[24] *Norges Offisielle Statistikk VII*, 81:72–79.
[25] *Norges Offisielle Statistikk IV*, 27:182; Semmingsen, *Veien mot Vest*, p. 468.

We cannot pretend that the evidence given by the district medical officers in their annual reports is conclusive proof that the returned emigrant was always an innovator or an improver. On the other hand, these medical officers were in a position to know their district and its people well, and this is certain: they found the influence from America noteworthy.

If the social readjustment taking place in Norway made conditions favorable for the impulses transmitted by the emigrants to take root and if the Norwegian immigrants adapted themselves with relative ease to the conditions of the rural communities of the Middle West, does it follow that emigration from other Old World countries had similar consequences? Did the contact prove most effective when the community of culture — of patterns of behavior — in the sending and the receiving country was most pronounced? Was the receptivity of the immigrant — his ability to interpret the conditions of the new land — and the receptivity of his public at home — its ability to make use of the impulses — greatest in these circumstances?

The process of adaptation, adjustment, and assimilation obviously was the more difficult for the immigrant the farther apart he stood from the traditional American pattern of life, the greater the difference in language, religion, political outlook, and everyday habits. An additional difficulty for the rural immigrants who settled in American cities was that they had to change from a rural to an urban way of life at the same time that they moved to a foreign country. Whether they were compelled to do so by economic necessity, whether they sought the cities because breaking new land was not the kind of agriculture they understood or because their conditions at home had left them with a distaste for farming, the urban way of life was an additional element of strangeness.[26] It seems reasonable to presume that these difficulties made the immigrant a less vigorous exponent of America and American ideas. And if we confine our interest to the motifs which, in the period 1840–80, were predominant

[26] Robert Ernst, *Immigrant Life in New York City, 1825–1863* (New York: King's Crown Press, 1949), p. 62; James P. Shannon, *Catholic Colonization on the Western Frontier* (New Haven: Yale University Press, 1957), pp. 50, 69, 126, 140–50, 167–71; Oscar Handlin, *Boston's Immigrants* (Cambridge, Mass.: Harvard University Press, 1959), p. 130 and *passim*.

in Norwegian America letters — political democracy and social equality — we may ask, first, whether immigrants coming from more static countries would stress these features of American society in their letters home, and second, whether reports of this kind would arouse the same kind of interest in all countries as they did in Norway. Perhaps the American example would not seem applicable in the same sense because conditions at home were too different. It is impossible to provide an answer to problems of this kind until the America letters of several European countries are collected and the impact of the contact with America studied in its various aspects.

It seems to me, however, that the messages sent home to his native village in Italy or Poland by an immigrant in an American city must have been alien, difficult to understand, and certainly difficult to apply to conditions at home and to translate into action. In these countries, the messages sent from America might act as a stimulus to increased emigration, while to those who remained behind they would seem like fairy tales. Perhaps the emigrant coming back to a static milieu would, if he remained at home, have to conform to the traditional pattern without being able to provide any impulse for innovation. Or, if he did not conform, he would be regarded as a "strange bird"; the people in the old country would see no reason for copying him nor would they have the opportunity of doing so. At least we may presume that impulses from America needed a longer time to make themselves felt in the economically and socially less developed and more static countries of southern and eastern Europe.

Let me illustrate my thesis with a few examples. It is reasonable to assume that the impact of contact with America through emigration was as great in countries like Germany and England as it was in Norway, possibly even greater. The picture of America Marcus Lee Hansen paints in his chapter "America Becomes the Common Man's Utopia" seems to point in that direction. True, Hansen was not concerned with the impact of emigration on those left behind, but he did write about the significance of the America letters. "The arrival of such a letter was not merely a family, but a community affair. Neighbors assembled, the schoolmaster was pressed into service, and the letter was read amidst a silence that bore eloquent testimony to the profound interest. Often copies were made and sent to other communities." He told of German book clubs which made a special study of America, of English farm servants and artisans reading inexpensive weeklies containing information about America, and of philosophers among the village clergymen and schoolmasters who "thought of America not only as a place of bigger farms and higher wages, but as a new country with a social mission divine in its origin." [27]

The centuries-old contact with her colonies gave England a special knowledge about and a special relationship to America. But in nineteenth-century England, too, this knowledge reached new social groups — the industrial worker, the farm servants, and the philosophically minded schoolmasters mentioned by Hansen — through the agency of mass emigration. Chartists, in the 1830's, looked hopefully to America and by 1840 correspondence between Great Britain and America was so extensive that single packet ships carried as many as 16,000 letters.[28] On the other hand we are told that English immigrants were hardly regarded as foreigners at all when they came to America. The language was no barrier and they were able to fit into the American environment more readily than any other immigrant group. The English industrial worker brought technical skill to American industries, and trade union traditions to the American labor movement. Until well into the second half of the nineteenth century the English newcomers were more nearly teachers than apprentices. The common ground they shared with Americans was wider than that held by any other immigrant group on the American scene.[29]

[27] *The Atlantic Migration* (Cambridge, Mass.: Harvard University Press, 1940), p. 170.

[28] Wilbur S. Shepperson, *British Emigration to North America: Projects and Opinions in the Early Victorian Period* (Oxford: Blackwell; Minneapolis: University of Minnesota Press, 1957), p. 10; Michael Kraus, *The North Atlantic Civilization* (New York: Van Nostrand, 1957), p. 71.

[29] Rowland T. Berthoff, *British Immigrants in Industrial America, 1790–1950* (Cambridge, Mass.: Harvard University Press, 1953), pp. 15–16, 35, 61, 65, 87, 125–29, and *passim*; Clifton C. Yearley, *Britons in American Labor, A History of the Influence of the United Kingdom Immigrants on American Labor, 1820–1914*, The Johns Hopkins University Studies in Historical and Political Science, Series LXXV, No. 1 (Baltimore, 1957), *passim*.

Writing about the extensive circulation of American newspapers in England in the 1850's, J. M. Ludlow observed: "As these newspapers came almost solely from the North, the foundation was laid of that marvellous sympathy of our manufacturing population with the North in the American war for the Union — a steadfast sympathy, based upon knowledge and combined with true insight — which held in check not only the Southern proclivities of our aristocratic and moneyed classes, but the indifference and self-interest of that portion of our working population which was not so directly connected with America."[30]

In England, the contact with America was so vital that even those without a vote followed English foreign policy during these critical war years with intense interest and managed to influence it. America was better understood in the cottage than in the mansion, wrote Trevelyan. Indeed, those who lived in the mansions not only knew little of America, they were even ignorant of the prestige of America among the common people in their country.[31]

It was John Bright who saw this most clearly, who understood the intimate relationship that existed between the lower middle and the working classes in England and their friends and relatives in the Northern States. Bright also understood the connection between the victory of the North in the Civil War and the future of the reform movement in England; his followers grasped this connection too, despite the pro-Southern sympathies of some old trade-union leaders, who did not want to concern themselves with politics at all, and of the press they controlled.[32] When Bright made his forceful attack on privilege at the Trade Union meeting in London in 1863, he had the future of both American and English democracy in mind. And his listeners, who were beginning to feel that they, too, had a "stake in the country," took a stand and made the cause of the Northern States their own. And so, in the words of H. C. Allen, "the cause of the

---

[30] *Atlantic Monthly*, 74:620 (November 1894).

[31] George M. Trevelyan, *British History in the Nineteenth Century and After* (London: Longmans, Green, 1938), p. 331.

[32] George M. Trevelyan, *The Life of John Bright* (London: Constable, 1914), p. 306: "Family ties bound many humble homes in England to the men who were fighting under Grant and to the women who were praying for their victorious return."

North came increasingly to be recognized for what it was, the cause of democracy, for this was of the greatest moment, since feeling for the North and joy at Northern triumphs became more and more associated with the movement for Parliamentary reform in Britain, and its future became closely bound up with the outcome of the Civil War. There is no doubt that the Northern victory greatly facilitated the passage of the Reform Bill of 1867." [33]

The history of these war years suggests that contact through emigration brought greatest results when the difference between America and the Old World was discernible, but not too great, when the beginnings of political democracy and social recognition existed in the old country, and when the general patterns of culture and ideas were common to both nations.

While the English middle and labor classes had a part in creating opinion and in influencing England's attitude toward an American problem, the Irish emigrant took his problems with him from Europe and concerned himself still more intensely with them after he had arrived in America. In the violent nationalistic outbursts in Ireland, the Irish-American played a considerable part, and although the anti-English sentiment in Ireland needed no inspiration from abroad, the support which the Young Irelanders, the Fenians, and the Land Leaguers received from the Irish in America was of no little importance in planning, organization, finance, and execution. In Arnold Schrier's words (on Young Ireland) "not only did money become the entering wedge of American influence . . . but personal leadership also came to be drawn from the United States, and the nationalist movement of the next generation found 'masses of eager supporters' among the incoming hordes of emigrants at a time when it had nearly expired on the 'auld sod.'" [34]

In this case, the immigrant group worked systematically to exert its influence on the political development in the home country. The Irish, more than most of the other European emigrants, had been

[33] *Great Britain and the United States: A History of Anglo-American Relations, 1783–1952* (London: Odhams Press, 1954), pp. 496–98; Royden Harrison, "British Labour and the Confederacy," *International Review of Social History*, 2(Pt. 1):78–105 (1957).

[34] *Ireland and the American Emigration*, p. 125.

pushed out, almost expelled, from their native land by the catastrophe of the potato famine or by miserable living conditions caused by the social system and by English policy. The hatred of England which they brought with them, and the difficult process of adaptation they had to undergo in America, are both factors of importance in shaping a contact which, significant as it was to the nationalist movement in Ireland, did not for a long time engage the passion of the Irish peasantry itself.

What influence did the letters from America, and the returned Yankees have on the rural masses in Ireland? According to Schrier's account, the news of high wages, social equality, and an uncomplicated way of life contained in the America letters had no effect other than to encourage emigration. The example of America seemed to have no relevance at all to conditions in Ireland. Irish farmers were conservative and bound by strong, traditional ties: it is typical that they wove the ceremony of parting on emigration into the old pattern of wakes, and instituted a special farewell ceremony, an American wake. It is interesting to note that cleanliness, a concern for hygiene, and industry are qualities found in returned emigrants in both Norway and Ireland, and that in both these countries, as well as in Italy, those who returned home used their savings to build new houses or improve the old. But while the Norwegian farmer was receptive to the ideas from abroad, the Irish farmer was, for a long time, immune to such innovations. "Some Yanks," writes Schrier, "did not hesitate to criticize their friends and relatives for lazy habits but all to no avail for the force of tradition was stronger than their most vigorous protests." And again: "As well dressed as the Yanks were and as hard as they worked to make improvements in their houses or on their farms, they nevertheless remained objects of curiosity and admiration; rarely did they become examples to be emulated." Even in the realm of political ideas "the Yank seems to have made no significant impression. If he brought any back with him, he appears to have kept them to himself." [35] This is a good example of a traditional, conservative milieu not receptive to the impulses which came from contact with America.

[35] *Ibid.*, pp. 134, 139–40, 141.

The history of Italian emigration also seems to confirm this. As far as I am aware, there are no collections or studies of America letters proclaiming the impression the new country made on the Italian immigrant. But in no other people was there such a crossing and recrossing of the Atlantic as among the Italians, and a number of *americani* went back to settle down in Italy. Some of them returned with a fair amount of money, though most of those who achieved real economic and social success stayed in America. The few of this category who did return did not invest their money in industrial or other business enterprises in Italy, but lived on their means, lent out money or property, and added up their dividends. America had left her mark on their clothes and their outward appearance, but their way of life and their social ambitions were determined by the social conditions of the home country.

Most of the returning *americani*, however, were workmen or peasants whose savings consisted of a few thousand lire. They, too, had achieved some social advancement and they were reluctant to work for wages after their return. If this became necessary, they preferred to return to America. In Italy many bought land with their savings. But, as they had not learned anything about agriculture in New York or in the other big cities, they never became innovators in Italian agriculture. "In truth it is a matter of regret, as one turns the pages of the parliamentary report upon the southern *contadini*, to find how general the tale is that improved methods had not been introduced by the returned emigrants." [36]

Instead they leased out land, if they were in a position to buy so much that this was possible; and they, too, could occasionally add to their income by lending out money. Many of them built new houses which, though hardly decorative, were in two stories and had a partition separating the animals from the family. "Sometimes, as in a number of communes of the Abruzzi and Molise, there are entire quarters that have grown up with the new abodes of the americani." [37]

[36] A. Sartorius, Freiherr von Waltershausen, "Die süditalienische Auswanderung und ihre volkswirtschaftlichen Folgen," *Jahrbücher für Nationalökonomie und Statistik*, Folge III, 41:1–27, 182–215 (see pp. 182–90); Foerster, *The Italian Immigration of Our Times*, pp. 453–54.

[37] Foerster, *The Italian Immigration of Our Times*, p. 457.

Apart from the pioneer work of Thomas and Znaniecki on the Polish peasant in Europe and America, the subject of emigration from eastern and southeastern Europe and its impact has barely been touched upon by scholarly research, and consequently we can only hazard the guess that these countries were not more receptive to the ideas that made up the old image of America than, for instance, Italy. Yet, historical processes take a long time to develop, and influences may have been at work and may have prepared the ground without producing visible results.

Let me turn once more to the example of Ireland and look at the economic and social transformation which began there in the last decade of the nineteenth century. This change made the Irish peasantry owners of the farms they worked, introduced a money economy into agriculture, and disrupted the old rural system. During this process, the Irish peasant gave up his traditional outlook. He discovered for the first time that industry and hard work might bring him profit, and that the opportunity to climb the social ladder existed for him, too. "Once people could profit by their industry or forethought, any addition to their material wants, any new channel of satisfaction might bestir the lazy, stiffen the feckless and compromise the selfless," says K. H. Connell and, enumerating the influences which helped to establish this notion of social ambition and self-improvement, he mentions travel and newspaper reading and continues: "but most vividly and consistently it was driven home by letters and visits from brothers and sisters living in America."[38] Here, too, once the movement began, the contact with America was a factor of importance. And the same may be true of Italian emigration. Even if it be true that the majority of the south Italian emigrants departed illiterate and returned illiterate, even if many of the returned lived in idleness upon their savings, the new houses they built, the new clothes they wore, the self-assurance they displayed — in common with returned emigrants from many lands — are signs, though perhaps only superficial ones, of a change which, in some cases, meant a new independence. Sartorius tells of the returned emi-

[38] "The Land Legislation and Irish Social Life," *Economic History Review*, Series II, 11:1–7 (August 1958), quotation from p. 4.

grant who refused to take off his cap to his employer; Foerster notes "a more resolute attitude toward the employing landlord" (a consequence, he adds, "of sterling, epochal value") and a higher standard of education.[39]

Emigration and contact with America through letters and visits insinuated the notion of change into the mind of the European peasant, and from this notion sometimes grew the ideas of social advancement, self-improvement, and progress, all preconditions of political and social democracy. Whenever such a movement got under way and gained impetus in the home country it was influenced by emigration and contact with America. The impulses so transmitted had helped to widen horizons and had implanted the prestige of America in the mind of the common man.

Here is a field worthy of research, yet one whose surface has barely been scratched. It is a subject which is accessible to the student of economic and social history, the student of the history of ideas, the sociologist, and the social anthropologist.

[39] Foerster, *The Italian Immigration of Our Times*, p. 459. A scholar who decided to investigate what this new attitude meant, for instance, to the Italian trade-union movement and to the labor movement might be able to find a connection here.

by PHILIP D. JORDAN

The Stranger Looks at the Yankee

Tʜɪꜱ ɪꜱ the simple saga of three men.[1]
One was a carpenter, one a smith and ironmonger, one a liveryman,
who got his start currying horses and renting teams. The first was
baptized Thomas Patrick Dailey, the second bore the name of Philip
Perlstrom, and the third was Frederick Wilhelm Unterkircher. They
came to the United States separately and without knowing one another. They arrived in the decades before the Civil War. Each lived
beyond fourscore years and each crossed the threshold of the twentieth century.

The lad from County Cork settled down to cut with saw and build
with nails and hammer. The young, towheaded Swede fiddle-footed
across the land, blacksmithing in lumber camps, shoeing government mounts at western cavalry posts, sowing wild oats — if the
yarns he spun can be believed — before establishing himself in the
same community where Tom Dailey was nailing on shingles and
putting up lath. The frugal German, as was not uncommon in those
days, turned a livery stable into an undertaking business. It was said
of him that his funerals always started on time.

When the three died, one by one and within a few years of one
another, the Irishman, mourned by children and grandchildren, was
buried from St. Patrick's Church, a poor church, indeed, which stood
slantwise on a hill just above the Murray Iron Works. The Swede,

[1] These are not fictional characters, although their names, for the purpose of this
paper, have been slightly altered. The author knew them well, was a frequent guest
in their homes, listened to them recite their American adventures many times, was a
pallbearer for one, attended the funerals of the others. Today he is friendly with their
children and great-grandchildren. One of the trio was the author's grandfather.

also mourned by children and their children, was carried gently to the Lutheran churchyard and placed in a green plot shaded by elms. The German, leaving loving sons and affectionate daughters, received the benediction of the German Methodist Church and was laid to rest not too far from the Lutheran cemetery and just across town from the Catholic burying ground. One found a final home in a box of pine, one in a sturdy coffin of oak, and one in a casket of polished walnut. Yet the same earth received them all.

Before they died, one by one and within a few years of one another, the Irishman's voice still was thick with the cream-rich brogue of his native land, the Swede spoke with a lilting inflection, the German maintained the flavorful pronunciation of the Rhineland. Dailey was devoted to whiskey, Perlstrom preferred wine, and Unterkircher drank beer the year round. Dailey was a bottom-drawer Irishman, Perlstrom struggled to lace-curtain respectability, and Unterkircher, achieving a measure of wealth and local fame, was a member of the middle-class aristocracy, not because he was an efficient layer-away of the dead, but because he had been elected mayor. Unterkircher drew solid votes not only from "Dutchtown," a community of laborers and artisans, but also from precincts and wards heavily populated with Irish and Scandinavian immigrants.

He got these votes because he was not a Yankee and because he was a good man, who furnished carriages free of charge to the Irish priest and the Lutheran pastor when they went to the beds of the sick and because never, in his whole, long life, did he enter a fee when his ambulance carried the injured to Mercy Hospital or St. Joseph's Hospital or the town hospital, which was nonsectarian. "'Tis a strange thing," mused the pastor of St. Patrick's, "that a German, and a Methodist at that, should be such a good man." "We can both be thankful," answered the Lutheran minister, "that he isn't an Episcopalian."

Grace Episcopal Church, it must be understood, was not only thoroughly Yankee in its membership, but was located on North Hill, a wealthy section dominated by residences of New England businessmen, bankers, and lumber merchants. North Hill was Snob Hill, and Snob Hill was far removed, indeed, from Dutchtown and from South

Hill, where Irish boarding houses catered to free-swinging Paddies. North Hill was even farther, in both spirit and distance, from Shanty-town, a miserable, jerry-built district lying between the railroad tracks and the great river. The few North Hillers, smug in prestige and morn-ing coats, who did not attend Grace Church gave their support to the First Congregational Church. It was of New England origin, for its first pastor, a man who dominated the pulpit more than half a cen-tury, had come west from Andover Theological Seminary during the early 1840's. Although tolerant, he had little use for frontiersmen and foreigners.

The slab of slate, the headstone of granite, the pyramid of marble betoken more than the quiet resting places of three strangers — one an Irishman, one a Swede, and one a German — who found a home and a share of security and happiness. The markers symbolize, not a statistic, but a way of life; not an equation in population trends, but an adventure in searching; not the American pursuits of three men from three different Old World cultures, but of all men from every-where who sought fortune and safety and liberty in a land where the people were sovereign and Manifest Destiny was king. The three headstones — one slate, one granite, one marble — are universal sym-bols of success and failure, of grandeur and meanness, of fairy tales come true and of those whose feet never fit the slipper. Most of all, when the symbol is raised to universal proportions, the three cemetery monuments mirror a thousand, thousand different images of Amer-ica.

When strangers, like the Irishman, the Swede, and the German, arrived in the land of their choice, they peered through spectacles of curiosity at America and its inhabitants. Their refractive indices were determined by a bizarre pattern of truth, half-truth, and myth. It is little wonder that resultant images on both eye and mind all too frequently were misleading and untrustworthy. The foreigner's atti-tude was conditioned by what happened to him, by what he saw, by what he thought he saw, by what others told him, and by what was withheld from him. Thus it was that truth was tinctured with imag-ination; that half-truths sprang from distorted accounts of what life in America really was as opposed to what propagandists pictured it to be; and that myths, as is the manner of all myth, fashioned themselves from a blending of ignorance, a smattering of legend, a wild tangling of fantasy with reality.

The stranger's view of the new home is reflected in an abundant literature. Laborers from the Old Sod, liberty-loving Germans, pietistic Scandinavians, excitable French — all these and more left their impressions. Catholics, Lutherans, Episcopalians, Methodists, and just plain heretics reacted in prose and verse. Both the articulate and the inarticulate began trickling into the United States not long after the close of the War of 1812. Within decades the trickle became a torrent. By 1860, when Dailey and Perlstrom and Unterkircher already were putting together a new destiny, the torrent was an ocean whose swells had inundated the East and were washing westward through prairie land, the savannas, the lake country, and on to El Dorado, where miners in red shirts still courted Lady Luck. Many a man, caught up in this tidal wave, sent "America letters" home; others rushed impressions into pamphlets and books; and some contributed to both foreign-language and English newspapers. The printing press became an overflowing cornucopia, spilling descriptions, prejudices, songs and ballads, essays in the art of bigotry, romantic and factual narratives, and columns of advice, both wise and foolish.

It was a pamphlet, stuffed with advice, that brought Thomas Patrick Dailey to America.[2] It first influenced him years after it was published, and he kept it as a prized treasure. It was found among his effects after his death, its torn pages tied with butcher string. The author of this paper-wrapped tract was Mathew Carey. Versatile economist, pugnacious editor, and himself a refugee from Ireland, Carey published his reflections on America in 1826. In that year he had lived in the land of promise for forty-two years, observing the American scene and feeling secure in his perception of the American character.[3]

[2] Mathew Carey, *Reflections on the Subject of Emigration from Europe* (Philadelphia: H. C. Carey and I. Lea, 1826).

[3] For biographies and comments, see *Dictionary of American Biography*, III, 489–90; Lea and Febiger, *One Hundred and Fifty Years of Publishing, 1785–1935* (Philadelphia: Lea and Febiger, 1935), pp. 5–20; Henry W. Boynton, *Annals of American Bookselling, 1638–1850* (New York: Wiley, 1932), pp. 127–38, 149–

Although Carey was correct enough when he warned that "no man, on any account whatever [ought] to cross the Atlantic to settle in the United States unless he be seriously disposed to industry and economy," he also perpetuated a prevailing half-truth.[4] Irishmen, like Dailey, learned they would not be obliged to crouch in subservience once they passed through the golden portals of liberty. Indeed, Carey, careless of fact, said that even the poorest of men could "stand erect and unawed" in the presence of any man, "whatever may be his grade, his station, or his wealth."[5] The Yankee nation, he continued, guaranteed strangers security of person, security of property, and security of worship.[6] Carey's romantic brush splashed bright and hopeful color on the canvas depicting a never-never Beulah land.

The curious fact is that, although Carey himself was confident that his appraisal of the national scene was valid and that security would, in fact, be the immigrant's cherished possession, there was no general agreement, even by Americans, on these issues. And many foreigners learned by bitter experience that Carey's promises were only partially accurate. The stranger had only to scan the newspapers of Carey's own City of Brotherly Love to learn that daily the mayor's court was jammed with unfortunates from abroad. And while the press seldom, if ever, mentioned that an American was arrested for larceny or drunkenness, it always emphasized, for example, that six sons of Hibernia were charged with rioting, that John Ray of the Emerald Island was drunk, that Johannah Gallagher, a "trim-looking" servant, was found intoxicated in a Philadelphia alley.[7] The Germans and the Irish read that they were kin to rapacious locusts.[8]

Many a newly arrived immigrant learned sorrowfully that he could not expect even reasonably satisfactory police protection. It mattered little if he settled in an eastern city or a western town. The less de-

---

51; Carl Wittke, *The Irish in America* (Baton Rouge: Louisiana State University Press, 1956), p. 63; and Mathew Carey, *Autobiographical Sketches* (Philadelphia: J. Clarke, 1829).

[4] Carey, *Reflections*, p. ix.

[5] *Ibid.*, p. 11.

[6] *Ibid.*, pp. 12–13.

[7] *Philadelphia Public Ledger*, March 25, 26, April 5, 1836. The *Ledger* was examined for the years 1836–50 inclusive and many similar examples were found.

[8] *Ibid.*, October 29, 1836.

sirable sections of New York, where thousands of newcomers were to put first roots, were lacking in law enforcement and were described as early as 1817 as localities stigmatized by intemperance, prostitution, theft, and gambling.[9] It was almost impossible for an immigrant seeking help to find a peace officer. "And," said a commentator, "look at their style of dress; some with hats, some with caps, some with coats like Joseph's of old, parti-colored. If they were mustered together, they would look like Falstaff's Regiment."[10]

Gangs of native rowdies, filled with liquor and armed with knives, nightly roamed avenues to assault and rob the defenseless. The Irishman was not the only drunk, and the German not the only thug. If law enforcement was a scandal in cities such as New York and Philadelphia, it was little more than a mockery in western communities. Cincinnati established a short-lived night watch in 1806, but a regular police force was not to come for decades.[11] As late as 1885, an Ohio governor said it was better for a boy to remain in reform school than to be released and "exposed to the temptations and evils of life in Cincinnati."[12] St. Louis still did not have a regular force in 1830.[13] Chicago did not maintain a satisfactory force until 1861.[14] And Columbus, Ohio, home of many Germans, put up with an inefficient department until at least 1873.[15] One of Unterkircher's first acts as mayor was to improve the motley watch he inherited.

[9] Ward Stafford, *New Missionary Field: A Report to the Female Mission-Society for the Poor of the City of New-York and Its Vicinity* (New York: J. Seymour, 1817), pp. 12, 13–14, 15; see also Robert Ernst, *Immigrant Life in New York City, 1825–1863* (New York: King's Crown Press, 1949), Chapter 4.

[10] J. W. Gerard, *London and New York: Their Police and Crime* (New York, 1853), pp. 6, 17–18; for an editorial on the inefficiency of the Philadelphia police, see the *Public Ledger*, August 11, 1836.

[11] Richard C. Wade, *The Urban Frontier: The Rise of Western Cities, 1790–1830* (Cambridge, Mass.: Harvard University Press, 1959), p. 89.

[12] Quoted in Philip D. Jordan, *Ohio Comes of Age, 1873–1900* (Columbus: Ohio State Archeological and Historical Society, 1943), p. 266.

[13] Wade, *Urban Frontier*, p. 290.

[14] Bessie L. Pierce, *History of Chicago, 1848–1871*, Vol. II (New York: Knopf, 1940), p. 310.

[15] Eugene H. Roseboom, *The Civil War Era, 1850–1873* (Columbus: Ohio State Archeological and Historical Society, 1944), pp. 46–47. For the rise of police protection in Minneapolis, see [A. E. Costell], *History of the Fire and Police Departments of Minneapolis* (Minneapolis: Relief Association Publishing Co., 1890), pp. 235–322. As both the frontier and the immigrant moved westward, the latter noticed

Perlstrom, the Swedish blacksmith, once reminisced that all too frequently the "land of the free" seemed to those from abroad to be a place where one apprehension was exchanged for another. Too many strangers, he said, learned they must bend their knees not only to prejudiced police and civil magistrates but also to shady bond brokers, crafty boardinghouse keepers, shantytown politicians, tenement-house owners who levied excessive rents, and runners of their own nationality who fleeced them. "But it didn't last forever, thank God," he added. No better account of the perfidy of the runner is found than that describing the plight of a bewildered Irish lad who stepped ashore at New York in 1848:

The moment he landed, his luggage was pounced upon by two runners, one seizing the box of tools, the other confiscating the clothes. The future American citizen assured his obliging friends that he was quite capable of carrying his own luggage; but no, they should relieve him — the stranger, and the guest of the Republic — of the trouble. Each [runner] was in the interest of a different boardinghouse, and each insisted that the young Irishman with the red head should go with him . . . Not being able to oblige both gentlemen, he could oblige only one; and as the tools were more valuable than the clothes, he followed in the path of the gentleman who had secured that portion of the "plunder" . . . the two gentlemen wore very pronounced green neck-ties, and spoke with a richness of accent that denoted special if not conscientious cultivation; and on his (the Irishman's) arrival at the boarding house, he was cheered with the announcement that its proprietor was from "the ould counthry and loved every sod of it, God bless it!"[16]

Year after long year, immigrants wrote and talked and complained of the dark side of American life. Many thought of themselves as babes in a democratic woods. Some interpreted America as a place where thieving hands stole their baggage;[17] where they seemed des-

increasing laxity in law enforcement. In 1880, the Reverend C. L. Clausen, traveling to Fort Pierre on business for the Norwegian-Danish Evangelical Lutheran Church in America, wrote that "saloons and gambling houses flourished and murderers were openly pointed out to the visitor" (quoted in Kenneth O. Bjork, *West of the Great Divide: Norwegian Migration to the Pacific Coast, 1847–1893* (Northfield, Minn.: Norwegian-American Historical Association, 1958), p. 375.

[16] Quoted in Ernst, *Immigrant Life*, p. 28.
[17] *New York Tablet*, November 20, 1858.

tined to everlasting poverty;[18] where the first words a child heard at school was the reproach, "You are a Dutch-Dutch Lizzie";[19] where every conceivable trick was played upon those whose ears took in, but did not understand, the common language.[20] Nor did they always comprehend American ways. A Norwegian explained that Yankees knew how to interject the appearance of law and order "even into a practice which in the nature of the case is the direct opposite of law and order."[21] Not even valiant efforts of emigrant benevolent societies could guarantee a meeting of minds and the prevention of hoodwinking and trickery.[22] "Is it not a fearful thought," said a sympathetic editor, "that such a fate awaits the pure and virtuous who bring their honest industry to our shores?"[23]

[18] *London Morning Chronicle*, January 5, 19, February 12, 1852.

[19] *European* (New York), December 20, 1856.

[20] George M. Stephenson, *The Religious Aspects of Swedish Immigration* (Minneapolis: University of Minnesota Press, 1932), *passim*; Einar Haugen, "Language and Immigration," in *Norwegian-American Studies and Records* (Northfield, Minn.), 10:1–43 (1938); Theodore C. Blegen, *Norwegian Migration to America: The American Transition* (Northfield, Minn.: Norwegian-American Historical Association, 1940), Chapter 3; Marcus L. Hansen, *The Immigrant in American History* (Cambridge, Mass.: Harvard University Press, 1940), p. 131. Examples of the "broken speech" ascribed to immigrants are found in William F. Kirk, *The Norsk Nightingale* (Boston: Small, Maynard, 1911), and in Oscar Handlin, ed., *Immigration as a Factor in American History* (Englewood Cliffs, N.J.: Prentice-Hall, 1959), pp. 138–40, where "The Good-Natured German" is reprinted from Charles F. Adams, *Leedle Yawcob Strauss* (Boston: Prang, 1878), pp. 119–22.

[21] Gunnar J. Malmin, ed., *America in the Forties: The Letters of Ole Munch Raeder* (Minneapolis: University of Minnesota Press, 1929), p. 77. Laurence M. Larson wrote in his *The Log Book of a Young Immigrant* (Northfield, Minn.: Norwegian-American Historical Association, 1939) on p. 68: "It is therefore not strange that he [the immigrant] came to believe that he was being exploited by the native businessmen, and often too the belief was well founded. Usury was a practice of which farmers complained most bitterly: in one case a helpless immigrant paid interest at the rate of fifty-five per cent." The pursuit of the material things, by fair means or foul, is touched upon in a variety of sources: *Blackwood's Magazine*, 69: 551 (May 1857); *Harper's Magazine*, 19:408 (October 1859); *Outlook*, 117:119 (September 16, 1917); Andrew J. Torrielli, *Italian Opinion on America as Revealed by Italian Travelers, 1850–1900* (Cambridge, Mass.: Harvard University Press, 1941), p. 97.

[22] *Boston Notion*, July 23, 1842. Only a "comprehensive and well-organized plan of emigration," said the London newspaper *John Bull*, in its issue of June 24, 1848, could help eliminate evils found in America. The *Morning Chronicle* of London urged, on March 19, 1850, that local associations collect funds for the "protection of the poorer classes of emigrants from the system of plunder and imposition . . ."

[23] *New York Tablet*, November 20, 1858.

The defrauding of immigrants, indeed, was so general that foreign-language and denominational newspapers deplored the wholesale swindling and characterized American cities as the most bribable, corruptible, thievish, and abject in all the world.[24] Nor was this all. Editors enumerated a variety of quarrels not only among groups of strangers but also between strangers and natives. "Pennsylvania," said an editor, "has its jealousies of political influence between Germans and non-Germans; New York the same between Dutch and non-Dutch; and several other states are to be cursed with Irish and Irish-American parties." Then he added smugly that only unity of language and a great preponderance of Englishmen and those of Anglo-American character had prevented such disputes from being carried to greater extremes.[25]

As the western states developed, editors urged immigrants to flee the East for the plains of Indiana, the good earth of Iowa, the advantages of Wisconsin and Minnesota, the wide-open spaces of Texas.[26] The Texan Land Company, in 1848, promised 320 acres to any respectable man and wife, with or without family, and 160 acres to single men of seventeen years or older.[27] Almost any locality, between New York and California, was preferable to a Yankee-dominated eastern seaboard. Strangers were urged to emigrate to Oregon, where there was room enough to dump all the kings of Europe and all their subjects.[28] And, as everyone knows, they did travel, forming knots of homeland culture the length and breadth of the land, establishing themselves corporately and individually, weigh-

---

[24] *Catholic Telegraph and Advocate* (Cincinnati), March 11, 1854; *Arbeiter Zeitung* (New York), September 10, 1864.

[25] *Philadelphia Public Ledger*, September 3, 1850.

[26] *Catholic Telegraph and Advocate*, March 2, April 20, 1850; August 19, 1854.

[27] *Newspaper* (London), February 26, 1848.

[28] *Catholic Telegraph and Advocate*, April 13, 1850. In the issue of April 13, 1850, the editor wrote: "A strong, active, industrious Irish workman might as well commence digging his own grave, as to shut himself up in one of our large cities. The misery, poverty, destitution, wretchedness, and starvation, witnessed in the large capitals of Europe, are to be met with equally in all the large cities of America. For a poor man to think of bettering his condition by coming to look for employment in New York, Philadelphia, Cincinnati, or New Orleans is only leaping from the frying pan into the fire . . . fly from the large cities as from a plague . . . The best inheritance, an Irish philanthropist, can bestow upon his countrymen, in, or about coming to America, is to warn them — to KEEP CLEAR OF THE CITIES."

ing America on the scale of hope, but balancing the hope with weights of reality. America, they found, was a land of contrasts.

Confused and disheartened by a complicated, not simple, social structure, the immigrant viewing America was baffled and irritated by nativist forces that ridiculed and made sport of his religion. Many learned to their regret, as did Dailey, that it was no easy thing to worship as they pleased. They met with prejudice both in city and country, in the East and in the West. In New York, a Presbyterian clergyman warned of the expanding strength of Catholics from Ireland and Germany.[29]

When the Irish carpenter and the German liveryman arrived in the same Iowa town, the pattern of prejudice and the bulwark of bigotry already were fortresses of hate. German Methodists and Lutherans were anathema to Congregational ministers, who wrote of them: "The tide is swelling that rolls in upon us, drifting to our shores an incalculable amount of infidelity, superstition, and error, which threatens to lay waste and destroy our institutions. Tens of thousands, soon to be increased to hundreds of thousands, of this class of foreigners reach our land annually and form a very important and influential element of our Western population."[30]

Germans, like Unterkircher, arriving in the Hawkeye State joyful in the hope of intellectual liberty and economic freedom, were characterized by Congregational snobbery as "sheep without a pasture" and as enjoying "in a very limited degree any of the divinely appointed means of grace."[31] Perhaps this is why, in the latter years of his life, the Irish carpenter who went to final rest in a plain, pine box was kidnapped by the Ku Klux Klan. Perhaps this humiliating episode was the end result of a climate of opinion expressed by a Boston

[29] William Bannard, *A Discourse on the Moral Aspect and Destitution of the City of New York* (New York: Scribner, 1851), p. 15.

[30] Quoted in Philip D. Jordan, *William Salter: Western Torchbearer* (Oxford, Ohio: Mississippi Valley Press, 1939), p. 107.

[31] *Ibid.* American society was split by other than religious differences. The *New York Herald* wrote, in its issue of May 23, 1849: "Within the last few years, it has been apparent to philosophers of all grades, from the most astute pundit of the Historical Society down to the reflective oyster-man of Fulton Market, that new and formidable barriers have been creating division and hostilities between the working classes and those who style themselves the exclusives of New York society."

merchant in 1846, who urged his Iowa son-in-law to encourage public education as an effective barrier to the spread of Romanism.[32] Perhaps this is why a recently published book that attempts to interpret the heritage of the Middle West emphasizes the contributions made by Protestant colleges and churches and gives scant credit, indeed, to the heritage left by non-Protestant denominations.[33]

Perhaps this, in part, is the reason why Dailey and Perlstrom and Unterkircher looked on New Englanders with suspicion and distaste, would never use the term "Yankee" except as a blasphemy, and, until their dying hour, refused to acknowledge that the American character was anything but an amalgam. Perhaps this is why the three saw North Hill and Grace Episcopal Church as representative of a "foreign" culture and an alien way of life. Swedish-Lutherans most certainly resented the proselyting techniques employed by Episcopal rectors.[34] There were times when Thomas Patrick Dailey would have agreed enthusiastically, although sadly, with a brother Irishman, who wrote from New Orleans: "I must say to you that for an Irishman this is no country anymore. Hostility to him and to his holy religion is now the order of the day with numbers of fanatical Americans."[35]

Even intellectual Unitarians, with their spirit of "natural friendliness," looked upon foreign immigrants with less than cordiality.[36] Amos Lawrence, leader in the New England textile industry and humanitarian philanthropist, resigned himself to the fact that immigration evils must be endured.[37] The Reverend William Ellery Channing, lecturing to the Mechanic Apprentices' Library Association of Boston, doubted if American workmen could stand their ground

[32] Philip D. Jordan, ed., *Letters of Eliab Parker Mackintire of Boston . . . to Reverend William Salter of Burlington, Iowa* (New York: New York Public Library, 1936), p. 18.

[33] John J. Murray, ed., *The Heritage of the Middle West* (Norman: University of Oklahoma Press, 1958), *passim*.

[34] Stephenson, *Religious Aspects*, p. 157.

[35] Quoted from the *Limerick Reporter* in the *European*, March 28, 1857.

[36] Octavius B. Frothingham, *Boston Unitarianism, 1820–1850* (New York: Putnam, 1890), Chapter 8.

[37] William R. Lawrence, ed., *Extracts from the Diary and Correspondence of the Late Amos Lawrence with a Brief Account of Some Incidents in His Life* (Boston: Sheldon, Lamport and Blakeman, 1855), p. 270.

against the "half-famished, ignorant" workmen from Europe, who, he said, would toil for any wage and would never devote an hour to personal improvement. Channing, with his usual eloquence, prayed that heaven might preserve the United States from closer relations with Europe. Separation should be accomplished, he urged, even if it "should require us to change our present modes of life, to narrow our foreign connexions, to desist from the race of commercial and manufacturing competition with Europe; if it should require that our great cities should cease to grow, and that a large portion of our trading population should return to labor . . ."[38]

Such attitudes, reflected in the press both at home and abroad, were to some degree responsible, during the 1850's, for a movement to divert Irishmen from the United States and to send them to Canada and to South America. The *Liverpool Times* reported that, in 1856, some 12,000 Irish already were in Buenos Aires.[39] The *London Times* explained why it was more advantageous to emigrate to South America rather than North America:

There is a hostile and detrimental influence, which was daily growing in force before the Know-Nothing party existed, and which will operate against European immigration long after that organization ceases to be heard of. It is painful and morally dangerous to the Irishman in the United States to find his religion persecuted and himself cast out from one settlement after another on account of his creed; but it is worse in every way to find himself despised, oppressed and subjected to overwhelming temptation on the ground of his being of the industrial class; and this is what the immigrant finds if he is misled into settling in the slave States for the sake of Catholic privileges, or of profits above the average; or if he goes so far West as to be drawn into the vortex of the strife about free and slave labor . . .[40]

Yet, in the same decade that diversion was suggested, an ebullient and garrulous Irish priest found America a happy land, a generous country anxious to open hospitable arms in welcome to workers and cotters from the Emerald Isle. This optimistic reporter was Dr. Daniel

---

[38] *Works of William E. Channing, D.D.* (Boston: J. Munroe, 1846), 5:225–26.
[39] Quoted in the *European*, November 15, 1856.
[40] Quoted in the *European*, November 22, 1856.

W. Cahill.[41] Trained in mathematics and astronomy and once editor of the spark-tossing *Dublin Telegraph*, Cahill arrived in New York in November 1859. A firm foe of England, he was a devout friend to his beloved countrymen. His affection for the United States was boundless. From the moment he landed until shortly before his death in Boston in 1864,[42] Cahill toured the United States and Canada, preaching, lecturing, and writing a long series of America letters. The correspondence was published not only in Archbishop John Hughes's *Metropolitan Record* but also in such papers as the *Catholic Telegraph and Advocate* of Cincinnati and, of course, the *Dublin Telegraph*. Addressed affectionately to the tenant farmers and laborers, Cahill's reports, although not as spritely in spirit as was the German Grund's interpretation of Jacksonian America,[43] were read eagerly. Not often, from the day he first glimpsed the wonders of New York until the outbreak of the Civil War, did Cahill desert his chosen theme: America is the ideal location. Like Carey before him, Cahill constantly argued that the humbler classes were elevated in the United States to a position of self-respect, moral dignity, and national importance.

In America, said Cahill, workers earned good wages.[44] In America, police protection was more than adequate.[45] In America, a drunken man was abhorred.[46] In America, tradesmen dressed as well as aristocrats.[47] In America, the Irish were industrious.[48] If, perchance, his countrymen had difficulty, it was of their own making. And if Irish servants had troubles with their mistresses, it was because the girls were inefficient domestics. The lasses should have been trained properly before leaving home. Cahill explained:

Being the daughters of laborers, or needy tradesmen, or perhaps rack-rented cotters, they are ignorant of the common duties of serv-

[41] For biographical sketches, see *Dictionary of National Biography*, VIII, 210, and the *Metropolitan Record* (New York), December 8, 1860.

[42] *Boston Daily Advertiser*, October 29, 31, November 1, 1864.

[43] Francis J. Grund, *Aristocracy in America* (London: R. Bentley, 1839); the first American edition of this volume was published as a Harper Torchbook (New York, 1959).

[44] Letter dated December 7, 1859.   [45] Letter dated December 14, 1859.
[46] Letter dated December 14, 1859.   [47] Letter dated February 15, 1860.
[48] Letter dated December 14, 1859.

ants in respectable positions. They don't understand the cleaning of glass or silver plate. They cannot make fires expeditiously, or dust the carpets, or polish the furniture. Many of them never saw a leg of mutton boiled or roasted. Several of them cannot even prepare their own dinner bacon or pork, from the miserable lot and inextricable poverty in which these creatures of persecution and of sectarian scorn have been steeped above the lips from the sad hour of their birth to the last agonizing moment of their wretched lives.[49]

From his comfortable room in the Astor House, Cahill recorded a society that pulsed with energy, that was full of promise, that was to achieve a triumphal destiny. He wrote that every American was aboard a "go-ahead national train." Where were they bound? Cahill supplied the answer:

They are all going to their respective callings, avocations, crafts, necessities, encouragements, adventures, to the various rivers, creeks, villages, towns, cities, diggings, lands, prairies, manufactures, in the different States of this boundless country. Increasing population; new towns, advancing factories, new mineral discoveries, new widening agriculture, progressing harbors, attract all classes of men to these new points of trade, progress, and civilization; and as these points are every day multiplied, there is a permanent migration through the whole Union to fill the wants of these rising, laboring, artisan, commercial, and professional positions. . . . England puts fetters and manacles on the limbs and arms of your national trade and advancement; while the American Republic adds vigor, muscle, and active practice to the encouragement of commerce and to the popular power.[50]

One might add also that Americans were rushing pell-mell into the greatest sectional struggle the nation has ever known. The Civil War, however, seemed to come as a surprise to Cahill. Yet his unawareness of the approaching conflict was not as significant as was his acceptance of the myth of the truly national character — a set of characteristics that marked every American and made most of them as much alike as the proverbial peas in a pod. Yet this error was not of his making. Cahill only mired himself, as others had before him and more were to do after him, in a tar pit of generalities.

[49] Letter dated December 20, 1859.
[50] Letter dated December 27, 1859.

The myth, so naively accepted, was simply structured. It affirmed that "the American" was unique, and it assigned peculiar characteristics to "the Yankee." This myth had been long in the making and was of New England origin.[51] It stemmed from the Brother Jonathan concept and eventually, after molding and shaping, was to emerge as Uncle Samism. Although Brother Jonathan and Uncle Sam mirrored a Yankee image, New Englanders were just as apt to refer to themselves as an Ephraim Snooks or a Clarissa Bumpkin or a Jeremiah Barnbeans. The image itself was as elusive as a shadow reflected in a shimmering pool. Not even men from New England could come to agreement on the common traits wrapped in the stereotype.[52] From 1815 until long past the Civil War, both Americans and foreigners debated the character of the American Yankee.[53]

It is true, of course, that the stranger was apt to call any American a Yankee, using the term both in praise and as a bad name.[54] To Gustaf Unonius,[55] the Yankee was a man possessed of inventiveness; to a young Norwegian, the Yankee was a "smart" one who preyed upon newcomers;[56] to still another immigrant, Yankees were those

[51] Philip D. Jordan, *Uncle Sam of America* (St. Paul: Webb, 1953); Mitford M. Mathews, *A Dictionary of Americanisms on Historical Principles* (Chicago: University of Chicago Press, 1951), II, 1793.

[52] Royall Tyler, *The Yankey in London* (New York: D. Longworth, 1809), pp. 75–76.

[53] William Dunlap, *Yankee Chronology* (New York: D. Longworth, 1812), p. 15; John Neal, *Brother Jonathan* (Edinburgh and London: W. Blackwood, 1825), I, 153–55; *Yankee* (Portland, Maine), June 11, 1828; *Yankee and Boston Literary Gazette*, January 18, 1829; *Yankee Farmer* (Boston), December 15, 1838; *Boston Daily Advertiser and Patriot*, August 1, 1838; *Lowell Mercury and Massachusetts Gazette*, July 30, 1831.

[54] See, for example, J. F. D. Smyth, *A Tour of the United States of America* (Dublin: Price, Moncrieffe, 1784), II, 230; *American Joe Miller* (Philadelphia: Carey and Hart, 1841), p. 91; Edward Stephens, *High Life in New York* (New York, 1843), *passim*; William E. Burton, *The Yankee amongst the Mermaids, and Other Waggeries and Vagaries* (Philadelphia: Getz and Buck, 1843), *passim*; John L. McConnel, *Western Characters* (New York: Redfield, 1853), pp. 276–77; Philip Paxton, *A Stray Yankee in Texas* (New York: Redfield, 1854), p. 266.

[55] Jonas O. Backlund, trans., and Nils W. Olsson, ed., *A Pioneer in Northwest America, 1841–1858: The Memoirs of Gustaf Unonius*, Vol. I (Minneapolis: Published for the Swedish Pioneer Historical Society by the University of Minnesota Press, 1950), p. 215.

[56] Larson, *Log Book*, p. 68.

who made sport of foreigners.[57] To some Irish, the Yankee was a "cool, calculating villain, with a great contempt for the Irish, and [with] a high opinion of his own ability and acuteness."[58] The editor of a German-language newspaper saw nothing in the Yankee worth emulating. Too many Germans, he said, imitated Americans and, by so doing, only made themselves ridiculous.[59] When a minor German novelist looked at the Yankee, he saw a tall, gaunt, sinewy fellow, whose clothes hung loosely, whose shoes were slit across the toes to give air and space to long feet, and whose vanity was made obvious by a watch chain of gold.[60] The descriptions are as many and varied as the men who wrote them.[61] Yet other observers saw Yankees as more than mean, grasping, calculating, and vain. "When the Yankees saw how hard we worked," sang a Norwegian emigrant ballad, "they were friendly and kind, and many there were who sent us food. God bless their generous souls."[62] The literature is replete with such evidence.

[57] Malmin, ed., *America in the Forties*, p. 16.

[58] *Brownson's Quarterly Review*, 17:118–30 (January 1860), gives much attention to the Irishman vs. the American in a review of Paul Peppergrass, *Mary Lee, or The Yankees in Ireland* (Baltimore: Kelly, Hedian, and Piet, 1860).

[59] *Arbeiter Zeitung* (New York), March 3, 1865. *Harper's Magazine*, 10:694 (April 1855) said in the Editor's Easy Chair: "The Germans are much inferior to the independent American citizen in many things, but the capacity of enjoyment is not one of them. That is one of the things in which Europeans generally are superior to him. . . . The Yankee can not play. If he goes to Rome and tries the Carnival, he flings handsfull of blinding *confetti* at every passenger, assuming that to be fun. . . . Jonathan must let the *fetes* and holidays go."

[60] Bjarne E. Landa, "The American Scene in Friedrich Gerstacker's Works of Fiction" (Unpublished Ph.D. thesis, University of Minnesota, 1952).

[61] "Yankeeism" was behind a comment in *Brownson's Quarterly Review* (17:255, April 1860): "The only way to guard against an ultimate injurious and destructive Americanism is to substitute in our ecclesiastical education the Roman cosmopolitanism, which can offend nobody, and which leaves the people free in every country to be Catholics, not Gentiles." A year later, Brownson had this to say: "If a Papist hand is more skillful in manipulating with the scalpel and dissecting knife, Yankees will not reject it and allow a disciple of Luther, Calvin, or Theodore Parker to hack and mangle their bruised limbs" (*ibid.*, 18:62, January 1861).

[62] Theodore C. Blegen and Martin B. Ruud, *Norwegian Emigrant Songs and Ballads* (Minneapolis: University of Minnesota Press, 1936), pp. 346–47. But on pp. 221–22 is found: "In Norway no one who begs a lodging for the night is turned away, but a self-made Yankee is less generous: it is every man for himself over there." The spirit of the older ballads is reflected in the songs of the newcomer today. Thus the Puerto Ricans sing: "I am going back to Puerto Rico even if I have

PHILIP D. JORDAN

A Minnesota German revealed his particular view of Yankee life
and manners in verse:

I do not like it in this
new Canaan. Whatever my
eyes beheld — it made me angry.
   The railroads go only at a crazy pace
   and you can hardly catch your breath;
   Beautiful nature flies by like in a dream,
   And that, certainly, is very disagreeable.

Before you go to the table
you almost die of hunger.
There are so many prepared dishes,
but only a few to my liking.
   The meat is full of blood
   and terribly tough;
   No matter how good your teeth,
   they will hurt
   And that, to be sure, is very disagreeable.

Of orderliness, peace and security
they know practically nothing.
Only a lot of murder and theft we
find in this new country.
   When you leave your home at a late hour,
   it is very easy to get into trouble;
   You will be attacked and robbed
   and perhaps you will be killed!
   And that, certainly, is very disagreeable.

No honesty exists here
in offices and politics.
Only ambition and avidity
rule the Republic.
   And if you have a legal fight
   with a wealthy person,
   I can tell you in advance, right now,
   that you are not going to win.
   And that, to be sure, is very disagreeable.

to go back swimming. There, even just eating bananas, I will go through life singing." (*Reporter*, 21:41 (October 1, 1959).)

The women, too, of this Republic
are very odd.
They talk about the happiness of married life,
but it is rarely true.

> Because, when the husband works from
> early to late and makes money,
> the wife spends it nonchalantly
> for dresses and ornaments.
> And that, certainly, is very disagreeable.

The temperance of Sundays
does not agree with me at all,
because the quintessence of life for me
is, and always will be, beer.

> Therefore, as far as America
> is concerned,
> I am full of it — up to the ears.
> Every Sunday I lose
> the nicest thirst,
> And that is very disagreeable.[63]

It is tempting, indeed, to quote similar examples which, directly or by implication, depict the stranger's view of the American in his native habitat. The intensity of New England cultural and economic imperialism, sensed if not discerned plainly by many a foreigner, is nowhere stated more clearly than in a Down Easterner's letter from California. Writing in 1848, the author commented enthusiastically upon the nation's rapid expansion and then said:

Louisiana, Florida, Texas, were once, and but a few years since, the territories of France and Spain. Ultra foreigners in language, birth, race, habits, manners, and religion! but now naturalized, fraternized — incorporated with that all-pervading solvent and amalgam, the universal Yankee nation. . . . Thus push we the bark of enterprise, adventure, conquest and commerce along, till we are fairly installed on the mountain heights that overlook the broad Pacific. Here am I, a confirmed emigrant, one of the foremost of that pioneer, pilgrim band, that starting from the North Atlantic shore, pursue the setting sun in his course. . . . This looks to me as the destiny of the Saxon, or Anglo-American race. If they fail to carry it out, it will be from

[63] *Minnesota* (St. Paul) *National Democrat*, October 23, 1858.

their losing a part of that roving, restless (and if it were not for the alliteration, I would say) resistlessly-reforming principle, that has hitherto impelled them to come in contact with everything and renovate everything they touched. So operative will be these national characteristics that California will soon be California no longer. The hordes of emigrants and adventurers (now or soon to be on their way here) will speedily convert this wild, cattle-breeding, lasso-throwing, idle, bigoted, bull-baiting race, into an industrious, shrewd, trafficking, Protestant set of thorough-going Yankees.[64]

Many immigrants, experiencing America for the first time, held, as did the young man in California, that there was a universal and nationalistic pattern of thought and action which could easily and accurately be expressed by the simple term "Yankee." Everything was Yankee and everybody was a Yankee. Such was not the case. Yet the conviction was deep rooted, and still lingers even today. And, curiously enough, some researchers have held steadfast to the belief that a national character — a set of traits marking the bulk of the people of the United States — was discernible in the 1820's and the 1830's.

Yet, in 1828, Timothy Flint, editor of the *Western Monthly Review*, challenged the concept of a national and universal character.[65] What the foreigner saw, said Flint, was a nation composed of peculiaristic regional types with each type imprinted with its regional mannerisms and attitudes. Flint, no doubt, might have admitted that New England Yankeeism was better known, but he would have been most unwilling to recognize New Englandism as a common denominator.

Flint spoke of the "distinctive" character of the French population, of the "marked nationality" of the Kentuckians, of men from Ohio and Indiana as possessing a character different from the character of natives in other western areas. He concluded that "among such an infinite variety of people, so recently thrown together, and scarcely amalgamated into one people, and in a country, where the institutions are almost as fresh and simple as the log houses, any very

[64] *American Agriculturist* (New York), 8:58–59 (February 1849).
[65] "National Character of Our Western People," *Western Monthly Review* (Cincinnati), 1:133–39 (1828); for a biography of Flint, see *Dictionary of American Biography*, VI, 474–75.

distinctive national character can hardly be predicted of the inhabitants."

Twenty-four years after Flint published his now little known essay, Thomas C. Haliburton discussed national traits. Haliburton made it perfectly clear that the term "Yankee" ought to be reserved only for residents from Down East. He also rejected the acceptance of a universal American character, saying: "The Eastern and Western, Northern and Southern States, though settled by a population speaking the same language, and enjoying the same institutions, are so distant from each other, and differ so widely in climate, soil, and productions, that they have but few features in common; while the people, from the same causes, as well as from habits, tastes, necessities, the sparseness or density of population, free soil, or slave labour, the intensity, absence, or weakness of religious enthusiasm and many other peculiarities, are equally dissimilar."[66]

Then Haliburton, as have more recent scholars, enumerated regional types. Each region, he pointed out, had a droll nickname, by which the character of its yeomanry, as composed of their ability, generosity, or manliness on the one hand, and craft, economy, or ignorance of the world on the other, could be known and illustrated. Thus, Haliburton continued, "there are the Hoosiers of Indiana, the Suckers of Illinois, the pikes of Missouri, the buck-eyes of Ohio, the red-horses of Kentucky, the mud-heads of Tennessee, the wolverines of Michigan, the eels of New England, and the corn-crackers of Virginia."[67]

A year after Haliburton struck hard against the concept of a universal national character, William Jerdan published in England a volume in which he noted essential differences between Texas and Virginia and between Georgia and Massachusetts.[68] In 1853, the very year in which Jerdan published, Joseph G. Baldwin differentiated between a thoroughgoing Yankee and a Westerner and added: "The Bostonian looks down upon the Virginian—the Virginian on the Tennesseeian—the Tennesseeian on the Alabamian—the Alabam-

---

[66] *Traits of American Humor* (London: Colburn, 1852), I, v.
[67] *Ibid.,* I, vii.
[68] *Yankee Humor and Uncle Sam's Fun* (London: Ingram, Cooke, 1853), p. 6.

ian on the Mississippian — the Mississippian on the Louisianian — the Louisianian on the Texan — the Texan on New Mexico, and we suppose, New Mexico on Pandemonium."[69] There was truth as well as waggery in the statement.

Discerning men also found deep cultural cleavages between the ignorant, poor Uplanders from the South and the better educated, more prosperous New Englanders. These differences the immigrant all too frequently failed to understand.[70] Yet the two types differed radically in almost every respect when they met in the midwestern states of Ohio, Illinois, and Indiana. Down Easterners brought with them a better knowledge of where to settle than did Uplanders; Down Easterners read better and wrote more correctly and more fluently; Down Easterners were better clerks because they ciphered better; Down Easterners exhibited more agricultural know-how; Down Easterners were the physicians and lawyers and newspaper editors; Down Easterners enjoyed a more adequate diet. "What'll you take," ran the old invitation, "wheat bread and chicken fixins, or cornbread and common doins?"

The Yankee introduced the straight-rowed, evenly spaced flint corn, and the inefficient carried with him the inferior southern gourdseed. The Yankee was aggressive and hard working, and the Uplander was passive and shiftless. The Yankee knew a place was reserved for him in heaven. The Uplander considered himself fortunate if he escaped hell by the width of a blister. In Ohio, the sentiment for publicly supported schools was especially strong in areas dominated by New Englanders. Only a child of Yankeeland could complete her sampler, as did a little girl from Down East, with the modest motto: "New England is my nation."[71] Perhaps the fundamental difference

[69] *The Flush Times of Alabama and Mississippi* (New York: D. Appleton, 1854), p. 223. See also Francis A. Durivage and George P. Burnham, *Stray Subjects, Arrested and Bound Over* (Philadelphia: Carey and Hart, 1849), p. 79: "There is a swarm of 'suckers,' 'hoosiers,' 'buckeyes,' 'corn-crackers,' and 'wolverines,' eternally on the *qui vive* in these parts . . ."

[70] The differences between the New Englander and the Uplander is ably presented in Richard L. Power, *Planting Corn Belt Culture* (Indianapolis: Indiana Historical Society, 1953).

[71] Dixon R. Fox, *Yankees and Yorkers* (New York: New York University Press, 1940), p. 2.

between the New Englander and the Uplander was expressed succinctly by a Frenchman, who declared that a Bostonian would "go in search of his fortune to the bottom of Hell" while a Virginian "would not go across the street to seek it."[72]

Many an immigrant, confused and baffled, imagined he saw a Yankee, when he actually was observing a Middle Westerner, a Southerner, or the man from Pike County. And many another believed he discerned a national character when he really was viewing only an untrustworthy and composite image. Then again — and all too frequently — it was fashionable to select a single trait, seize upon it, and elevate it, by extension, to a characteristic common to all, or most, Americans. Thus, for example, did David Macrae, a traveler, emphasize American boastfulness and practicability as national characteristics. He wrote in 1870:

Every State, every city, every village in America boasts of something. Massachusetts boasts of her brains; Pennsylvania of her oil wells; Virginia of her illustrious men; Alabama of her cotton; Louisiana of her sugar; California of her big trees; Missouri of her iron mountains; Illinois of her boundless farms; Kentucky of her horses; Canada of her incomparable wheat. . . . Philadelphia has the longest and straightest streets, and the largest orphanage in the country; New Orleans has the smoothest drive and the biggest river trade; Milwaukee has the best bricks; New York the finest park and the largest population; Boston has the best schools and the biggest organ; Chicago has the biggest saints, the biggest sinners, and the biggest pig-killing establishments in America.[73]

Such an affirmation sounds plausible. Yet it by no means strikes off a resounding whole truth, even though it is authentic in part. It fails to recognize, for example, that, even though many Americans talked big about physical achievements, there were others who spoke quietly and with humility of life in terms of values. There were those, in a score of sects, who, like the villagers of the Amana groups, were "remarkably quiet, industrious, and contented."[74] There were others

[72] Felix de Beaujour, "Sketch of the United States of America at the Commencement of the 19th Century," *North American Review*, 2:83 (January 1815).

[73] *The Americans at Home* (New York: Dutton, 1952), pp. 15–16.

[74] Charles Nordhoff, *The Communistic Societies of the United States, from Personal Visit and Observation* (New York: Harper, 1875), p. 43.

who, by nature, were not braggarts. Nor is it true that mobility was a universal trait of *the* American. Even Marcus Lee Hansen erred when he wrote in one of his delightful essays that the migratory habit was an "instinct." And Hansen was confused as to the meaning of the term "Yankee." He used it to mean the native-born, but a little reflection shows that even this interpretation is incorrect.[75]

Another interpreter, writing of the nineteenth-century American, said that Americans created folk heroes, such as Paul Bunyan, on a grand scale.[76] He ignored the fact that the now ubiquitous Bunyan was no product of the nineteenth century and most certainly was not a genuine folk hero. Indeed, he was a fake. If a folk hero catches up and represents values cherished by a people, then Johnny Appleseed is a better example than is Bunyan. Johnny Appleseed's modest and quiet exploits appeared in the public press in 1853.[77] Dignity as opposed to ostentation and quietness as opposed to exaggerated boasting were commented upon in *Harper's Magazine* in 1860. The comment was then made that preposterous vanity was no longer in vogue and that the eagle, the noble bird "we have chosen for our symbol shows more majesty by folding his wings in repose than in forever stretching them in weary flight."[78] Three years earlier *Harper's* spoke of the "composite mind" of the American.[79] As late as 1891 a Frenchman wrote that, although there were Americans in plenty, "*the* American has not made his appearance as yet."[80]

It is little wonder, then, that immigrants like Thomas Patrick Dailey, Philip Perlstrom, and Frederick Wilhelm Unterkircher saw many Americas and numerous Americans; that reliance upon easy generalization, the stereotype, and the myth was responsible, in part, for the failure of both strangers and natives to understand the complexity of national characters and manners; that, for the immigrant, comprehension was hampered further by the language barrier, by

[75] *Immigrant in American History*, pp. 61, 61–62.

[76] Henry S. Commager, *The American Mind* (New Haven: Yale University Press, 1950), p. 6.

[77] Robert Price, *Johnny Appleseed: Man and Myth* (Bloomington: Indiana University Press, 1954), p. 279, footnote 1.

[78] *Harper's Magazine*, 22:117 (December 1860).

[79] *Ibid.*,15:692 (October 1857).

[80] Max O'Rell, *A Frenchman in America* (New York: Cassell, 1891), p. 138.

inadequate securities, by nativist forces, by inability or unwilling-ness to see diversity rather than conformity, by emotion rather than by objectivity. The Irish carpenter, the Swedish blacksmith, and the German undertaker sensed what Whitman knew: "Here is not merely a nation, but a teeming nation of nations."[81]

[81] *Harper's Magazine*, 21:264 (July 1860), expressed the same view: "In fact, our people are so various in blood and breeding as to present specimens of almost all the manners and customs on the globe. . . . At the same time we are one nation, and are developing our national manners . . ."

by JOHN T. FLANAGAN

The Immigrant in Western Fiction

WHEN Crèvecoeur in 1782 attempted to define an American, he stressed the absence of titles, of church domination, of hereditary aristocracy in the New World. But in his composite picture he considered more than political conditions. To him Americans even in the late eighteenth century had multiple origins. Not only were they different in race and culture, but many of them were impoverished wanderers who literally had no country. For them the New World provided a spiritual and economic rebirth. In Crèvecoeur's famous words, "*He* is an American, who leaving behind him all his ancient prejudices and manners, receives new ones from the new mode of life he has embraced, the new government he obeys, and the new rank he holds."[1] Free in a new milieu, this American immigrant could act on new principles and therefore form new opinions and ideas. Self-interest motivated his actions; a comfortable existence was his reward.

A century and a half later another perceptive Frenchman, Father R. L. Bruckberger, claimed that the chief difference between the citizens of the Old World and those of the New was that the European was steeped in aristocratic tradition and theological discipline, whereas the American "believes only in political and social facts."[2] Here then is the classic contrast: the authoritarianism of the Old World and the pragmatism of the New. Variously motivated by economic serfdom, by the threat of starvation, by the arrogance of the aristocracy, by personal friction, and by the lure of adventure,

[1] *Letters from an American Farmer* (New York: Boni, 1925), p. 54.
[2] *Image of America* (New York: Viking, 1959), pp. 241–42.

the men who came first in driblets to America and then in a deluge were impelled by the passionate desire to substitute freedom for tyranny, whether that tyranny was social, ecclesiastical, or political. Oftentimes they came to grief, or triumphed vicariously only in the second generation; occasionally they even became backtrailers; but the lure persisted and instead of dimming grew stronger in the century following the American Revolution.

Curiously enough, in the relatively short history of the American novel the immigrant was slow to appear. Like the farmer, who became important in fiction only after a majority of the American people were classified as urban dwellers, he failed to capture the imagination of our early novelists. Immigrant protagonists indeed were rare before the rise of literary naturalism within our own century. This is not to say that foreign-born characters were excluded from our literature. But the portraits were often hostile and satiric. In the early native drama the Frenchman was usually a dangerous seducer and the Englishman a fop or a prig. British officers in the novels of Cooper were military trespassers, and in the tales of Hawthorne the royal governors were notoriously arbitrary and tyrannical. If the characters were not presented as villains or antagonists, their alien birth was so common as to cease to be a distinguishing mark. The principal figures of *The Scarlet Letter* were all of English nativity, but their place of origin had little to do with the moral and spiritual problems in which they were involved. Certainly it would be easy to identify characters of foreign birth in our nineteenth-century fiction from Queequeg in Melville's *Moby Dick* and the German socialist Lindau in Howells's *A Hazard of New Fortunes* to the Italian twins in Mark Twain's *Pudd'nhead Wilson* and the African prince Bras-Coupé in Cable's *The Grandissimes*. But collectively they were visitors or transients, and clearly they faced none of the problems peculiar to the later immigrant. Immigrant fiction, as we know it today, could not have existed before the flood of transatlantic migrants reached our shores after the Civil War and spoke in a babel of tongues which identified both their origins and their difficulties.

It would be futile to try to select the first immigrant novel no matter how loosely one ventured to define the term. Hjalmar H.

Boyesen's *Falconberg*, published in 1879 and dealing with a Norwegian settlement in Minnesota, might serve as well as any.[3] But this awkwardly told story of politics and temperance is artistically negligible. Also, to establish priority, one would need to survey the large number of novels originally written in Norwegian or Swedish or Danish or German, often published only in newspapers of limited circulation, and still untranslated.[4] The audience for such works was small, and the novels themselves were generally crude and hortatory. They have rightly been forgotten. In the last years of the nineteenth century, however, the newcomer was growing familiar as a subject if not yet memorable as a character, and within our own time immigrant heroes and heroines have become increasingly familiar. Indeed, because of economic, social, occupational, religious, and especially language barriers, their problems have remained special and for this reason their portraits, when sharply etched, are memorable.

It might be well at this point to differentiate among the novelists who have ventured to depict immigrant figures. In the first place, there are the foreign writers who visited or even lived briefly in the United States and who selected an American locale for their fiction. Charles Dickens devoted part of a long novel, *Martin Chuzzlewit*, to Ohio Valley scenes but was interested less in the real problems of the settlers than in venomous satire of the crude manners and the avarice of the backwoods. The Austrian Karl Postl (who used the pseudonym Charles Sealsfield) and the German Heinrich Balduin Möllhausen spent some time on the frontier and utilized their experiences in a number of romances; Möllhausen has even been called the German Cooper. Knut Hamsun, who worked as a laborer in the North Dakota wheatfields and as a streetcar conductor in Chicago, wrote short stories about the Middle West but never chose to devote a full-length novel to the scene. His countryman Johan Bojer, how-

---

[3] New York: Scribner, 1879.

[4] According to Theodore C. Blegen, as early as 1874 a writer named Nicolai S. Hassel published a novel "Alf Brage" in the periodical *For hjemmet* and followed it with a sequel in the same journal, "Raedselsdagene." Neither story ever appeared in book form but both dealt with the life of Norwegian immigrants in Minnesota. See *Norwegian Migration to America: The American Transition* (Northfield, Minn.: Norwegian-American Historical Association, 1940), pp. 586–88.

ever, wrote a novel called *The Emigrants* in which he pictured a Norwegian colony in North Dakota and gave close attention to the problems of social adjustment. More recently the Swedish writer Vilhelm Moberg has traced the migration of a group of settlers from Småland to Chisago County, Minnesota, in the 1850's. In a novel also called *The Emigrants* he explained the factors motivating the departure of his characters, and in a sequel entitled *Unto a Good Land* he told in earthy detail their experiences from disembarkation in New York to the choice of farmland in the St. Croix Valley.

A second and much larger group of writers includes those who were born in Europe and came to the United States either in infancy or in early maturity; when they turned to the writing of fiction they naturally utilized their own cultural groups as themes and sometimes, as in the case of O. E. Rölvaag, even employed their native language.[5] Familiar examples are H. H. Boyesen, Waldemar Ager, Martha Ostenso, and Rölvaag himself, all Norwegian-born; Sophus K. Winther, a native of Denmark and author of a trilogy about Danish settlement in Nebraska; David Cornel de Jong of Dutch nativity; Louis Adamic from Croatia; Stoyan Christowe of Macedonian origin; Anzia Yezierska, born in Poland; Ludwig Lewisohn, a native of Berlin; and Elias Tobenkin, Sholem Asch, Charles Angoff, and Abraham Cahan of Russian-Jewish birth. Other nationalities appear in their fiction, of course, but they chose to limit their novels' chief characters to the racial stock of which they were representative.

Finally, there are the American-born writers who, because they were second-generation members of immigrant families or grew up in a locality in which immigrant groups were conspicuous, have concerned themselves in their fiction with immigrant characters and themes. The success of their work is obviously due in large part to their literary skill, yet it is also related, one feels sure, to their sympathy toward and understanding of the difficulties of the alien.

[5] I am disregarding here works of fiction dealing with Spanish-Mexican immigrants in the Southwest or with Orientals on the Pacific Coast since these are relatively few in number and artistically inferior. Problems of Chinese and Japanese settlement in the Hawaiian Islands, however, occupy considerable space in James A. Michener's recent long novel *Hawaii* (New York: Random House, 1959).

Among such writers are Stuart Engstrand, Phil Stong, Frederick Manfred, Herbert Krause, August Derleth, Jo Pagano, Nelson Algren, Herbert Quick, Arnold Mulder, and Upton Sinclair; while on a somewhat higher literary level there are William Saroyan, Ruth Suckow, and Willa Cather.

In some of the fiction treating of immigrants, of course, the immigrants are not central but are merely part of the milieu. This is surely true of Phil Stong's *The Iron Mountain*, a novel dealing with various north European miners in a Mesabi Range community. Likewise in Martha Ostenso's *Wild Geese* the settlement includes Icelandic, Finnish, and Swedish farmers, but all are subordinated to the tyrannical figure of Caleb Gare, a Yankee farmer who drives his family to the point of rebellion. Young Jake Vandemark, the protagonist of *Vandemark's Folly* by Quick, is an orphan of Dutch descent who comes driving a herd of ill-assorted stock to frontier Iowa. But his difficulties and his triumphs have little to do with his nationality. Frequently, too, the problems of the immigrant and those of the proletarian worker are indistinguishable, and the plight of the wage slave in the garment factory or the steel mill becomes basically economic. Then we have the intensely felt protest novels of Upton Sinclair, Ernest Poole, I. K. Friedman, Robert Cantwell, and particularly Michael Gold, whose strident *Jews without Money* was a notable demonstration of East Side penury in 1930.

The reader of such works of fiction will quickly perceive that the place of origin of the writers is far less significant than their attitude toward character and scene. Basically it is their awareness of common immigrant problems that links them together. Save for the English and Irish who crossed the Atlantic — and there is little fiction of importance which deals with the life of these newcomers — the prospective citizens faced strikingly similar difficulties. Most of the immigrants were poor, timid, lonely; they were often badly informed about conditions in the land which they intended to adopt as their home. They had been reared in a different cultural tradition, and they frequently represented a different religious background from that of their new neighbors. Moreover, they were often poorly equipped for the work they wished to take up (as when Norwegian fishermen or Swedish millwrights or Czech tailors strove to become prairie farmers). One special limitation they all too obviously shared — the language barrier. Yet they were determined to achieve economic independence, and they yearned for social acceptance. When the novelist Anzia Yezierska was accused by critics of always playing upon the same theme, she did not deny the charge. "My one story is hunger," she admitted. "Hunger driven by loneliness."[6] The ways in which the immigrants overcame the obstacles imposed by a new society, or died in the effort to do so, account for the interest and variety of the fiction which portrays them — as unique a body of literature as can be found anywhere.

The new arrivals who lingered in the neighborhood of Ellis Island faced the same hardships and endured the same deprivations which had become familiar in their homelands. Jews from the grimy villages of White Russia or from the Warsaw ghetto generally stayed on New York's East Side and eked out a bare living as pushcart peddlers, sweatshop employees, or wage slaves in the garment industry. Crowded into noisome tenements, they were often evicted by greedy owners whom they looked upon as American Cossacks. Some, of course, by accident, determination, or superior intelligence rose out of the crowd to prestige and affluence. Fanya Ivanowna, the heroine of Anzia Yezierska's *All I Could Never Be*, finally establishes herself as a writer after many rebuffs but never wins the social acceptance she craves. In Elias Tobenkin's *Witte Arrives* another Russian immigrant wins a precarious economic foothold through journalism in Chicago and eventually makes his way back to New York. The parents in Myron Brinig's novel *Singermann* make a living in a Montana mining town, but it is their children who eventually win acceptance. The classic account of this kind of success story is Abraham Cahan's *The Rise of David Levinsky*, in which the young protagonist by bitter toil and indomitable self-restraint rises to wealth as a manufacturer of women's suits. As a character Levinsky is admirably drawn. He has the persistence and the fortitude to cope with all the economic problems that confront him, yet his material success

[6] *Children of Loneliness* (New York and London: Funk and Wagnalls, 1923), p. 18.

is empty, and in the end he finds no more genuine contentment, no more spiritual satisfaction, than Dreiser allotted to Sister Carrie.

The Czech and Scandinavian immigrants who pushed on to the Middle West, on the other hand, found obstacles different but not less formidable. Like the Jews in New York City they met an unfamiliar environment, strange faces, and a foreign tongue. Many of those who homesteaded in the Mississippi Valley had never been agriculturalists, and even those who were experienced in wresting a living from the soil knew little about prairie farming. The endless, treeless land and the sweep of the wind terrified them. The reader can never forget the anguished feeling of Rölvaag's Beret Holm that the immense Dakota landscape provided not a single tree to hide behind.

Novels devoted to the development of western land are rich and diversified in their characterization. Some of the immigrants were nostalgic and fearful, uncertain about the rightness of their decision, constantly pulled by memory or tradition. To adapt the term of Hamlin Garland, they became psychological backtrailers, and even if their malaise did not always impel them to return to their fatherland, they lived their lives in an atmosphere of fear and regret. Even those who were fugitives or rebels at home did not cut their ties completely and had many a poignant memory of what they had sacrificed. Thus Chris Schwietert in Ruth Suckow's novel *Cora*, a German tailor who could not continue his occupation in a small Iowa town, is neither a competent farmer nor a contented factory employee. Kindly in temperament and musically inclined, he remains a misfit. Nils Vaag, in Rölvaag's *The Boat of Longing*, is a poet and dreamer who recalls Norwegian song and folklore and prefers playing on his violin to working in the North Woods or on the Great Northern Railroad. Old Shimerda, in Willa Cather's *My Ántonia*, takes his own life in a fit of despondency and because he is a suicide is denied burial in the Catholic cemetery. These of course are the victims. On the other hand, there were scores who faced the future with confidence, secure in their conviction that nothing in the New World could be worse than their plight in the Old. The narrator of Stoyan Christowe's fictional autobiography, *My American Pilgrimage*, remarked when he was taunted about being a simple track layer: "I may carry steel for a while and live like a gypsy a summer or two. In the Old Country it's plowing and poking donkeys till you die."[7]

This indispensable faith of the pioneer in success has been well analyzed by George Santayana. Reflecting on the nature of the settlers in North America, Santayana observed that all the immigrants, with the exception of the Negroes, were voluntary exiles and that the American accordingly was the most adventurous or the progeny of the most adventurous of the Europeans: "It is in his blood to be socially a radical, though perhaps not intellectually. What has existed in the past, especially in the remote past, seems to him not only not authoritative, but irrelevant, inferior, and outworn. He finds it rather a sorry waste of time to think about the past at all. But his enthusiasm for the future is profound; he can conceive of no more decisive way of recommending an opinion or a practice than to say that it is what everybody is coming to adopt. This expectation of what he approves, or approval of what he expects, makes up his optimism."[8] Born in Madrid, a member of the Harvard University philosophy department for many years, and a resident of Italy when he died, Santayana had a unique opportunity to observe the behavior and adjustment of the immigrant to North America.

Years ago Percy Boynton observed that Rölvaag in *Giants in the Earth* had presented the classic contrast of the two main types of immigrants: the lusty, boastful extrovert in Per Hansa, the sensitive, fearful, suspicious introvert in Beret Holm.[9] Per Hansa gloried in the challenge of the New World, took things in his stride, exulted in his strength and ingenuity, became a natural leader of the small colony of transplanted fishermen, and boldly confronted the prairie gods. Beret, conscience-stricken by her surrender to Per before wedlock and by her desertion of family, church, and fatherland, turned neurotic and hovered on the brink of insanity. It is the great dramatic irony of the novel that the husband, ideally equipped for the new

[7] *My American Pilgrimage* (Boston: Little, Brown, 1947), p. 170.

[8] *Character and Opinion in the United States* (Garden City, N.Y.: Doubleday, 1956), pp. 104–5.

[9] *The Rediscovery of the Frontier* (Chicago: University of Chicago Press, 1931), pp. 126–34.

life, perished in a blizzard on a futile quest for a minister, and that his wife, inadequately prepared for the role of matriarch which was suddenly imposed upon her, was destined to survive until a third generation was on the threshold.

But if Per Hansa and Beret are the paradigms, they are not the only examples of first-generation homesteaders in American fiction. Casper Kaetterhenry, of Ruth Suckow's novel *Country People*, Peter Grimsen, of Sophus K. Winther's *Mortgage Your Heart*, and Alexandra Bergson, of Willa Cather's *O Pioneers!* have an equal will to succeed and reveal comparable energy and determination in their route to their goal. Kaetterhenry in Iowa and Grimsen in Nebraska acquire profitable farmland by dint of rigid self-denial and constant, grueling toil; moreover, they tyrannize over their families until they alienate their children. Worn out by endless work, Mrs. Kaetterhenry dies of cancer, whereupon her husband offers ten dollars to anyone who will find him a marital replacement. Grimsen, reminiscent in several ways of Haskins, the victimized renter in Hamlin Garland's famous short story "Under the Lion's Paw," feels the financial power of banker and landlord and resents their exploitation of the immigrant farmer. Alexandra Bergson, the Swedish-born daughter of a Stockholm shipyard worker, wins out as much by courage and intelligence as by hard work although it must be added that she also benefits from the good fortune which Willa Cather often bestowed upon her heroines.

A somewhat different success story is told by Elias Tobenkin in his novel *God of Might*. In this story Samuel Waterman, a Jewish merchant, establishes himself in Nebraska's capital city as the owner of a profitable department store and finds wealth but not social acceptance. Waterman experiences many of the reverses and frustrations familiar to David Levinsky although he is never given the full-dimensional depiction which Abraham Cahan accorded his protagonist. Whereas Levinsky hovers midway between two worlds, Waterman is inclined to revert to his orthodox heritage under pressure of an alien society.

It is obvious that the fictional homesteaders like the actual immigrants were primarily concerned with what Rölvaag called the landtaking. Occupying their acres, erecting some kind of shelter, plowing the soil, and planting a crop — these were the things that came first. The struggle was intense, and industry, endurance, and fortitude were sovereign virtues. Equally obvious is the great pride in the land. Fred Ferguson in Ruth Suckow's *The Folks* thinks back a generation and more: "Well, anyway, it was good land. His father hadn't made any mistake about that. It was good land, and they had owned it for a while, worked it, and received its benefits. This belief in the goodness of his native soil lay underneath the tottering structure of business faith, religious faith, everything. Whatever folks might do with it, the land was here. That was good."[10] And Alexandra Bergson relates the land to the future. "'How many of the names on the county clerk's plat will be there in fifty years? I might as well try to will the sunset over there to my brother's children. We come and go, but the land is always here. And the people who love it and understand it are the people who own it — for a little while.'"[11]

If the original settlers did not always make the transition from one continent to the other with ease and success, their children — at least in fiction — were almost uniformly prosperous. Willa Cather's Rosicky, the Bohemian farmer who was more competent than most of his neighbors, died of a heart attack but not before he had seen his son establish himself on a nearby farm and marry a town girl. Ruth Suckow's Kaetterhenry family quickly become substantial citizens who can look with pride on their solid buildings and their mechanical contrivances. Even the German farmers of Herbert Krause's stories of western Minnesota, *Wind without Rain* and *The Thresher*, improve their lot despite ignorance and a stubborn resistance to new ways of doing things. If the rural folk of Garland's *Main-Travelled Roads* rarely escaped from crushing poverty and the clutches of loan sharks, the second-generation immigrant farmers do not find such problems insoluble.

The difficulties involved in the landtaking were basic but by no means singular. The immigrants almost simultaneously faced other

[10] *The Folks* (New York: Farrar and Rinehart, 1934), p. 720.

[11] Willa Cather, *O Pioneers!* (Boston and New York: Houghton Mifflin, 1929), pp. 307–8.

problems which were social and spiritual rather than economic. The reality behind the mask was hard to penetrate, or as Stephen Vincent Benét put it,

> Never the running stag, the gull at wing,
> The pure elixir, the American thing.

Peder Victorious, the son of Per Hansa and Beret Holm, rebels against the Norwegian cultural tradition and grows interested in politics. The final stage of his revolt is symbolized by his marriage to an Irish Catholic girl, a marriage which is shortly wrecked by temperamental conflicts as well as by the religious differences between them.[12] Beret herself, firmly orthodox during her long life, consistently holds the absence of spiritual solace more important than the struggles to earn daily bread. Eric Jansson's colony of Bishop Hill in Illinois is the subject of Stuart Engstrand's novel *They Sought for Paradise*, and here the economic adjustments are subordinated to an account of the religious and sexual experiments of a group of Swedish immigrants. Some of the newcomers were of course resentful of the attempts of the orthodox church of their homeland to control them and repudiated this authority with bitterness. In David Cornel de Jong's *Belly Fulla Straw* the power of the Dutch Reformed Church becomes a kind of strait jacket from which many of the Hollanders strive to escape. And in such novels of the Dutch settlers in Michigan as Frederick Manfred's *The Primitive* or the fiction of Arnold Mulder, the dominies who crossed the Atlantic to act as shepherds to their flocks are pictured as inflexible, stolid, and often rapacious.[13] Another kind of involvement is illustrated by Park Leary, the Irish-born editor of William Ready's *The Poor Hater*, who gets mixed up in both politics and religion and is killed by opponents who resent his efforts to transplant Irish farmers to the Red River Valley.

Thus the problems of church and school, of temperance and social

[12] O. E. Rölvaag, *Peder Victorious* (New York: Harper, 1929).

[13] Frederick Manfred (writing under the pseudonym Feike Feikema), *The Primitive* (Garden City, N.Y.: Doubleday, 1949). Arnold Mulder wrote four novels of Dutch life in Michigan; perhaps the best known are *The Dominie of Harlem* (Chicago: McClurg, 1913) and *The Outbound Road* (Boston and New York: Houghton Mifflin, 1919).

adjustment, which troubled the actual immigrants are reflected in the fiction portraying them. And always there was the special problem of language. As Henry S. Lucas remarked of the Dutch settler in Michigan, "The barrier of language strongly influenced the education he gave his children, the kind of literature he read and wrote, and his religious and church life."[14] The first-generation Germans of Ruth Suckow's fiction never achieved complete identification with their region because of a double failure to understand and to communicate. Teutonic immigrants to the Wisconsin River Valley, as chronicled in the novels of August Derleth, lived more happily because they formed a homogeneous group. Emigrating or at least settling as a colony, the Germans around Sac Prairie retained many of their traditional customs and were contented with a fairly free intellectual life.[15] The Scandinavians who came to Wisconsin, Minnesota, and the Dakotas tried to preserve their linguistic as well as their cultural heritage and for a time achieved the bilingual culture which Rölvaag hoped might be permanent. But the original Swedish or Norwegian could not hope to escape the attrition of time. If, as Einar Haugen pointed out, some of the attempts at fusion were both illogical and ludicrous, the triumph of English as the single language was inevitable.[16]

The Russian and Polish Jews who swarmed into New York's East Side probably remained culturally homogeneous for a longer time, but the literature in which they appear is full of stories of their attendance at language schools and their sincere joy in speaking the first few English words. Not many of the figures in the novels reflecting their plight feel the *joie de vivre* of Leo Rosten's Hyman Kaplan, who studs his name with asterisks and makes a mishmash of several tongues, but their troubles were no less acute. Such an autobiography as Mary Antin's *The Promised Land* yields additional proof of the

[14] *Netherlanders in America* (Ann Arbor: University of Michigan Press, 1955), p. 579.

[15] August Derleth has written many volumes of verse and prose about the Wisconsin River Valley and his native community of Sauk City; a typical novel is *Shadow of Night* (New York: Scribner, 1943).

[16] See Haugen, "The Confusion of Tongues," Chapter 4 of *The Norwegian Language in America: A Study in Bilingual Behavior* (2 vols.; Philadelphia: University of Pennsylvania Press, 1953), I, 53–73.

difficulty of personal adjustment. The reverse of the coin, of course, is illustrated by the American tourist today who, suffering from poor linguistic training in the schools, is too often guilty of fractured French or German or Italian.[17]

At this point it is well to note that many of the American novelists of our century have slighted the immigrant theme and that some of the most gifted midwestern writers have all but ignored it. Sherwood Anderson was much more aware of the psychological and sexual problems of his characters than he was of their racial origins. One of Theodore Dreiser's most memorable portraits is that of Old Gerhardt, the German *émigré* who tried to preserve his native tongue and his dogmatic Lutheranism yet found it impossible to control his American-born family. But if the people of Dreiser's fiction are frequently German in origin, their problems have much more to do with their plight as wage earners victimized by a greedy capitalism than with their position as immigrants. Sinclair Lewis refrained from satirizing the German and Scandinavian farmers he often introduced into his early stories and indeed in *Arrowsmith* gave heroic stature to the German Jew Dr. Max Gottlieb. Yet his focus was usually on other themes than the special situation of the immigrant. One of the most gifted of recent novelists, Wright Morris, although he often writes about a Nebraska which does not seem too remote from the state that Willa Cather knew, is concerned mostly with such subjects as loneliness, personal isolation, and the desire for affection.[18] In the work of none of these writers is the immigrant central or even specially significant.

Louis Adamic once asserted that of all the immigrant novels which he knew, three stood out: *The Rise of David Levinsky, Giants in the Earth*, and *My Ántonia*.[19] There are good reasons for this judgment. In the first place, the best fiction portraying the immigrant is remarkably close in fact to the life of the novelist himself. The strong-

---

[17] An amusing anecdote concerns the American woman who, thinking she knew French, called out to the engineer of a boat train as it pulled out of a Paris depot, "Stop! stop! Je suis gauche derrière."

[18] Cf. Wright Morris, *The Home Place* (New York: Scribner, 1948), and *The Works of Love* (New York: Knopf, 1952).

[19] *My America* (New York: Harper, 1938), p. 187.

ly autobiographical tinge to the work of Rölvaag, Cahan, Anzia Yezierska, and many others ensures a genuine emotional involvement. If the protagonist and the narrator are never identical, they still share experiences and a point of view. Adamic's own novel, *Grandsons*, is an excellent case in point since his personal life in America provided both plot and locale and since his characters were descendants of a Carniolan miner who lived first in Montana and subsequently in Chicago.

Again, the incidents of the story are likely to be those observed by the novelist himself. His memory is more useful here than his imagination. The outsider can rarely feel the loss of a tradition and the clash of cultures as intensely as the immigrant who has personally experienced the uprooting. If the novelist is not himself a newcomer, he can often substitute for the actual experience personal acquaintance and social proximity. Thus the Armenians of William Saroyan's California stories are usually his relatives or friends. Ruth Suckow, daughter of a Congregational minister in Iowa, lived in many rural parishes and knew intimately the German farmers who populate her stories. Willa Cather, brought to Nebraska at the age of eleven, was quickly aware of the divergent groups in that prairie state and studied the French, Swedish, and Bohemian settlements. The very technique of two of her novels, in which she casts herself as the young male observer of the action, testifies to the close link between the writer and his material. Likewise, James Farrell grew up with the Chicago Irish of his stories and can frequently be identified with his hero, Danny O'Neill, the studious boy who does not end his life in the gutter but devotes himself to sports such as baseball and goes to the university.

Finally, in the novels which Louis Adamic preferred, it is the psychological complexities and the dramatic narrative which focus the attention, not the possible utility of the books as social propaganda. Characterization is given full value, and characters in tension sustain the reader's interest.

Unfortunately, many of the novels dealing with immigrant Americans are chiefly criticism of an economic system. The writers, for obvious and understandable reasons, resented the exploitation of cheap labor, the grasping landlords, the wretched working conditions, the social barriers, the lip service to democracy. Obsessed with the widening rift between classes which Henry George made his subject in *Progress and Poverty*, they produced analysis or indictment rather than fiction. Certainly most novels about immigrants in the United States not only fail to reach a high artistic level but often tend to be a part of proletarian protest literature — especially if published in the 1930's. Too many of the writers who chose to present Italian bricklayers, Slovenian steelworkers, or Polish buttonhole makers were, like Upton Sinclair, interested primarily in social documentation. In *The Jungle* [20] Sinclair employs the Lithuanian immigrant Jurgis as a human vehicle for his attack on the system which makes the packinghouse workers live like animals, dirty, diseased, and helpless. The workers are presented with telling impact, it is true, but the author's chief interest is his excoriation of economic slavery. After Jurgis's conversion to socialism, Sinclair's novel becomes an intellectual tract with little artistic value. [21]

The theme of *The Jungle*, incidentally, underscores another point. Most of the novels concerning immigrants have naturally dealt with the worker, the artisan, the farmer; there is hardly any fictional treatment of the immigrant intellectual. Professional men — lawyers, doctors, engineers, teachers — were of course not numerous during the first tide of immigration. Their status in their homeland was obviously secure and their income relatively stable. But especially after World War I more and more professional people emigrated and eventually enriched the artistic and intellectual life of the United States. Their struggles to adjust and to establish themselves in the New World have seldom attracted novelists.

An interesting recent exception is the novel called *Pnin* by Vladimir Nabokov, better known as the author of *Lolita*. Professor Timofey Pavlovich Pnin has come via Paris to America and has eventually found a teaching post at Waindell College in New England. Attempting to interest students in the language and literature of Russia some

[20] New York: Doubleday, Page, 1906.
[21] Walter B. Rideout, *The Radical Novel in the United States, 1900–1954* (Cambridge, Mass.: Harvard University Press, 1956), pp. 35–36.

years before the surge of interest in Russian studies, Pnin has extremely small classes, which he teaches ineptly. He is a man of narrow culture without a sense of humor, and his lectures to both students and public groups are handicapped by his failure to master English idiom or pronunciation. Moreover, because of departmental politics he has no real place in the college setup and eventually is squeezed out as the result of a feud between the chairmen of the French and German departments. Nabokov's portrait of the ill-adjusted professor is both sympathetic and satiric. Timofey Pnin is a memorable character in his own right; as a symbol of a group of expatriated scholars and teachers who never become fully at ease in the New World, he is particularly significant.

But even in the familiar area of the immigrant worker in an urban setting, many themes remain untouched. Foreign-born Americans have found employment as waiters, clerks, janitors, and seamstresses; they have taken places in factories and on the assembly lines; they have formed little islands of their indigenous cultures in the metropolitan life which swirls around them. Often they organize *vereins* or *eisteddfods* to preserve their native social life or their musical traditions. Newspapers published in their original tongues symbolize the link with the Old World although these tend to diminish in number and importance. Occasional national holidays, like the Irish St. Patrick's Day or the Norwegian Syttende Mai, serve to bring together both first- and second-generation immigrants and permit the planning of parades and picnics. In all this manifestation of the survival of traditions and especially in the constant social and personal adjustments required by the dominant society into which the immigrants have entered, there is ample material for the writer of fiction. Unfortunately only a few novelists have grasped their opportunity.

Competent writers have discovered the possibilities of Chicago as a theme and have made impressive contributions to literary naturalism. One thinks of Willard Motley's *Knock on Any Door*, of Richard Wright's *Native Son*, of Nelson Algren's *The Man with the Golden Arm*, of James Farrell's Studs Lonigan trilogy. Indeed the Italians, the Negroes, the Poles, the Jews, and the Irish of America's second city have been superbly handled in fiction. Chicago is not the only midwestern city of importance, however, nor is it the only one with large sections of foreign-born and bilingual population. Although the immigrant stream has tapered off considerably, there are still annual increments to the working force of Detroit, Cleveland, Milwaukee, Minneapolis, St. Louis, and Duluth. For most of these urban areas, fictional chroniclers have yet to appear and sympathetic but accurate interpretation remains to be made. The immigrant group in the large midwestern city is still a rich, a colorful, and a tempting subject.

Perhaps what we need is a new Rölvaag, whose native tongue is Hungarian or Finnish or Greek, and who can bring to the theme of the city the knowledge and insight which the Norwegian-American novelist revealed in his account of the settling of the prairies. Instead of a glorification of the husbandman there will be a tribute to the industrial worker. Indeed the new magnum opus might appropriately be called "Spacemen in the Sky." And if such a novelist should arise, one may be sure that his protagonist will not be a Per Hansa, whose frozen body was revealed when the spring sun melted an ice-encrusted haystack, but rather an urban giant whose chief task it will be to drop the penthouse of a Frank Lloyd Wright monolith on its hinges so that the moon can pass by unscathed.

by CARLTON C. QUALEY

Immigration as a World Phenomenon

THE field of immigration studies has until recently been primarily focused upon the United States. This has been a natural development because of the huge and dramatic transatlantic migrations and because the American people have been highly conscious of their immigrant ancestry. On the other hand, emigration studies have been peripheral to the nationalistic preoccupations of European historians who have treated the vast exodus, if at all, chiefly as an extension of national history. The fact that the emigration of millions of Europeans constitutes a major chapter of European history has largely escaped the attention of European historians. This astonishing myopia is now fortunately being corrected in small but growing degree. For the first time in its history the International Congress of Historical Sciences in 1960 scheduled a session on migrations.[1] The entire program of the seventh congress of the International Economic Association was devoted to international migrations.[2]

The broadened interest in immigration studies has brought with it a shift of emphasis in interpretation. Instead of directing attention largely to immigrant-receiving countries, such as the United States, investigations are turning toward the countries of emigration, chiefly in Europe, with special attention given to vital statistics of population growth and movement and to the consequences of industrialization. Attention is also shifting from preoccupation with migration to the

[1] Frank Thistlethwaite, "Migration from Europe Overseas in the Nineteenth and Twentieth Centuries" in *Rapports* of the International Congress of Historical Sciences, 1960 (Stockholm: Almqvist and Wiksell, 1960), V, 32–60.

[2] Brinley Thomas, ed., *The Economics of International Migration* (London: Macmillan, 1958), hereafter cited as Thomas, *Economics*.

United States to consideration of migration to other colonial areas and within Europe itself, not to speak of the movement of the peoples of Asia and Latin America. In other words, immigration study is becoming a world-wide field.

The distinctive feature of world migrations in the four centuries before World War I was the absorptive capacity of underdeveloped areas, especially in the Western Hemisphere.[3] The movement of vast numbers of people, primarily Europeans but also Africans and Asiatics, to underdeveloped areas, such as the United States in the nineteenth century, meant enormous stimulation of productivity (especially in regions capable of capital investment), consequent population increase by further immigration and by natural increase, and continuous fluidity in the character of cultures. The migrations were a vital part of the dynamism of the Western world. Out of these movements and changes have come new nations, new patterns, strong repercussions upon older civilizations, and revolutionary alterations in the structure of world politics.

As far as large-scale shifts are concerned, a period of stability would now appear to have been reached. This will mean amalgamation of peoples within each area and gradually some uniformity of cultural patterns. There would seem to be occurring a time of settling down, of crystallization, of conservatism in almost every meaning of the term. Is it not ironic that the immigration restriction policy of the United States, designed to safeguard national security, may very well operate in the opposite direction? A healthy, expanding economy needs new people and new ideas and cross-fertilization of all kinds. This has been true of growth in the past.

[3] This essay is based on material in the following: Thomas, ed., *Economics*; Simon Kuznets and Ernest Rubin, *Immigration and the Foreign Born*, Occasional Paper 46 (New York: National Bureau of Economic Research, 1954); W. F. Willcox, *International Migrations* (2 vols.; New York: National Bureau of Economic Research, 1929, 1931); D. R. Taft and R. Robbins, *International Migrations* (New York: Ronald, 1955); Brinley Thomas, *Migration and Economic Growth* (Cambridge, Eng.: Cambridge University Press, 1954); Conrad and Irene B. Taeuber, *The Changing Population of the United States* (New York: Wiley, 1958); E. P. Hutchinson, *Immigrants and Their Children, 1850–1950* (New York: Wiley, 1956); Harry Jerome, *Migration and Business Cycles* (New York: National Bureau of Economic Research, 1926); Maurice R. Davie, *World Immigration* (New York: Macmillan, 1936).

The major population movements in modern times have been (1) the largely voluntary migration of Europeans to underdeveloped areas, (2) the transfer of several million Africans involuntarily to the New World, (3) the movement to unoccupied lands by Asiatic peoples, especially Chinese, and (4) the transfer or transplanting of millions of Germans, Poles, Russians, Arabs, Hindus, Moslems, and other refugees to new national areas. Within these broad categories are innumerable regional shifts of population, which are governed primarily by economic forces but may also be influenced by political changes, religious factors, and catastrophes such as famine, disease, and war.

The movement of people from one country or region to another has been affected by a variety of conditions, but most such migrations have in common certain factors which may be summarized as follows:

1. The variations in vital statistics of areas of emigration have a delayed reaction of fifteen to twenty-five years in the emigration or lack of emigration. That is, there has been much variation in terms of real increase of population (births minus deaths plus immigration minus emigration), a good deal of variation in concentrations in the fertile age range of the population (18–35), and a steady increase in medical efficiency and consequent decline of disease and deaths (for example, few major plagues have occurred in modern times). When real population increase became heavy in any year or years, heavy emigration followed a generation later.

2. There has been overpopulation of agricultural areas, especially those lacking conveniently accessible industrial labor markets. The majority of people who emigrated in modern times came from rural village economies which had reached a point of labor saturation in terms of land and employment available. Where capital investment brought industrial development in countries of emigration, the flow of people from rural areas was diverted from emigration to migration into cities; this occurred notably in western Europe. However, the attraction of seemingly unlimited cheap and even free lands in underdeveloped countries overseas tended to sustain the flow of people to those areas even while industrialism came to the homelands.

3. The lateness of development of industrialization and urbanization in the countries of emigration delayed those countries in developing the capacity to hold their populations. Capital increment, industrialization on a large scale, and urban growth sufficient to maintain markets for mass production came to northwestern Europe chiefly after 1870, while they came slowly if at all to southern and eastern Europe. This meant that until very late in the nineteenth century, the governing economic factors were agricultural, with all the latter's weaknesses as to capital formation and powers of retaining population. Only since World War I has industrialism come to large areas of eastern Europe, chiefly under conditions of authoritarian collectivization and of restrictions on free movement of people. In many areas of southern and eastern Europe, industrialization has progressed slowly in any case. That industrialization and rapid capital increment can absorb and hold population has been spectacularly demonstrated by the West German Republic since World War II, a country that has not only recovered from devastating destruction and defeat but has absorbed some 12 million refugees into its population.

4. The expansion of relatively cheap transportation services, on land and sea, promoted mobility over long distances. A vital chapter of the story of world migrations has been the role played by railroads, highways, canals, seaports, steamship lines, and ultimately air transport. As long as emigration was served only by winding roads and cart tracks feeding into few and scattered seaports served by few and small ships, the flow of emigrants had to be small. As the seaports pushed connections into the hinterlands of western Europe and later to southern and eastern Europe, the tide of emigration rose to record proportions. With mass transportation came lowered unit costs, and an emigrant could manage to get to America for something less than fifty dollars.

5. As the underdeveloped areas began to contribute to world agricultural production, prices of agricultural products dropped, causing severe reactions in the already hard-pressed village economies of Europe. Protection in the form of agricultural tariffs came too late to help much where tried. To this massive undercutting of

their livelihood there could be only two answers: emigration or migration to the cities.

6. As foreign investment moved into underdeveloped areas, a labor market was created, and this new labor in turn created new capital which stimulated further immigration, especially if the underdeveloped area possessed raw materials capable of processing into steel and other essentials for an industrial economy. The obvious example of such rapid development is the United States. As long as such raw materials for industrialization were lacking, as in Latin America, for example, development was slow and immigration was limited.

7. As emigration got under way, and was sustained by availability of lands or by a labor market in the underdeveloped area, reports came back to the country of emigration through immigrant letters which formed a vital communications link. Enclosed in envelopes or transmitted by bank drafts were a growing number of remittances, reaching millions of dollars per year in some areas. These paid for the transportation of additional emigrants, stimulated transportation services, incited these services to new competitive efforts, and salved the wounded feelings of government officials who deplored the loss of thousands of people from their countries.

8. As the volume of emigration reached large proportions, a psychological factor appeared, loosely called "emigration fever," which carried hundreds and thousands along who would under normal circumstances probably never have left their homelands.

9. Throughout the migrations, the variations of flow tended to be in terms of the variations in migration of capital to underdeveloped areas. Emigration tended to follow capital migration, while increased investment at home tended to diminish emigration. There was therefore a direct relationship between capital movements, emigration, and business cycles.

10. There has been a return flow of migrants from the country of immigration to that of emigration, ranging from negligible numbers of Norwegians to nearly 40 per cent of the Greeks. In the Far East, these "birds of passage" are even more characteristic of the movement of peoples, whether seasonally or after several years away. Until

recent times, most of these movements were not carefully checked and recorded, and hence statistics are not as reliable as one would wish.

Of the major population movements mentioned earlier in this essay, the greatest was the emigration of more than 50 million Europeans, most of them since 1815 to the New World. The establishment of the European colonial empires in the sixteenth, seventeenth, and eighteenth centuries involved relatively small-scale emigration. For example, in 1763 the total non-official white population of South Africa was only 13,842.[4] In 1790, after two centuries of immigration and natural increase, the total white population of the thirteen original states of the United States was 3,172,006 and the Negro population was recorded as 757,208, making a total of 3,929,214.[5] Of the whites, the estimated percentages by country of origin were English, 60.1; Scotch, 8.1; Ulster Irish, 5.9; south Irish, 3.6; German, 8.6; Dutch, 3.1; French, 2.3; Swedish, 0.7; Spanish, 0.8; and unassigned, 6.8.[6] The total number of French and mixed French-Indian in French America in 1763 was not over 70,000, and there were about 15,000 Huguenots in the English colonies.[7] A restrictive emigration policy and a monopolistic land system resulted in only small emigration of Spaniards to Spanish America, while Portuguese Brazil remained an almost completely undeveloped land during the colonial period. Numerically, the largest population transfer in the colonial period was that of Negro slaves from Africa to the New World, especially in the century from the assiento of 1713 to the cessation of the United States slave trade in 1808.[8] Emigration from Europe to Far Eastern regions was under the control of national trading companies of the several nations involved, and it was confined to company and military personnel.

During the wars of the late eighteenth and early nineteenth cen-

[4] H. M. Robertson, "South Africa," in Thomas, *Economics*, Chapter 12.

[5] U.S. Bureau of the Census, *Historical Statistics of the United States, 1789–1945* (Washington, D.C.: Government Printing Office, 1949), p. 25.

[6] American Historical Association, *Annual Report, 1931* (Washington, D.C., 1932), p. 124.

[7] Carl Wittke, *We Who Built America* (New York: Prentice-Hall, 1939), p. 30.

[8] Estimates range up to 10 million, but there are no reliable statistics. Cf. U. B. Phillips, *American Negro Slavery* (New York: D. Appleton, 1918).

turies, emigration from Europe was reduced to small and uneven numbers. It has been estimated that from 1775 to 1815 about a quarter-million came to America.[9] The year 1815 marked the beginning of a new era as Europe turned from the Napoleonic wars to peaceful pursuits.

European emigration in the century after 1815 has all the qualities as well as the quantity of a great exodus. From the British Isles (including Ireland), it is estimated that more than 20 million people departed for overseas destinations — about 13 million to the United States, 4 million to Canada, and 1.5 million to Australasia.[10] More than 5 million Germans emigrated between 1843 and 1910, mostly to the United States, and to these should be added those who left earlier and came later.[11] From 1876 to 1914, about 14 million were recorded as having emigrated from Italy, chiefly to the United States, Argentina, and Brazil.[12] After 1815, 2 million left the Scandinavian countries of Norway, Sweden, and Denmark, with still others from Finland and Iceland.[13] Nearly a million left Poland,[14] and over 1.5 million Jews fled from eastern Europe.[15] One could go on citing figure after figure illustrating the emigration of portions of every national group on the continent of Europe, but enough has been said to demonstrate the volume of the folk movements.

The specific expulsive forces that operated to drive all these people out of Europe were these: (1) the prevailing rural poverty of the village economy of Europe, (2) the impact on agricultural Europe of industrialization, (3) the barbarities of labor conditions in the

[9] Marcus L. Hansen, *The Atlantic Migration, 1607–1860* (Cambridge, Mass.: Harvard University Press, 1940), p. 77.

[10] Julius Isaac, "Great Britain," in Thomas, *Economics*, p. 65.

[11] Hilde Wander, "Migration and the German Economy," in Thomas, *Economics*, p. 198.

[12] Robert F. Foerster, *The Italian Emigration of Our Times*, Harvard Economic Studies, no. 20 (Cambridge, Mass.: Harvard University Press, 1919).

[13] Theodore C. Blegen, *Norwegian Migration to America, 1825–1860* (Northfield, Minn.: Norwegian-American Historical Association, 1931); Eric W. Fleisher and Jörgen Weibull, *Viking Times to Modern* (Minneapolis: University of Minnesota Press, 1954).

[14] Wittke, *We Who Built America*, p. 420.

[15] Rufus Learsi, *The Jews in America: A History* (Cleveland and New York: World, 1954); Oscar Handlin, *Adventure in Freedom: Three Hundred Years of Jewish Life in America* (New York: McGraw-Hill, 1954).

new, raw industrial towns, (4) the prevalence of political inequalities among the masses of the population in contrast to the privileged classes, (5) the pietistic rebellions against the state churches and the rise of new sects, such as the Mormons, (6) direct religious persecution, such as that against the Jews, (7) compulsory military service, (8) the promotional activities of agents of steamship companies, (9) the effectiveness of the emigrant letters, (10) the influence of returned emigrants, as tangible proof of the advantage of emigration, (11) the increasing number of emigrant guidebooks to overseas territories, especially the United States, and (12) the "herd instinct" which took hundreds of families and individuals along with the groups, people who by themselves would not ordinarily have had the courage to tear themselves away from accustomed environments.

The attractive forces that drew people out of Europe were (1) land hunger and the knowledge that there existed millions of acres of rich farming land in the American and Canadian west, Australia, New Zealand, Brazil, and Argentina, (2) a continuous labor shortage in the underdeveloped lands, especially in those areas, such as the United States, to which capital was migrating, (3) the attractiveness of more liberal constitutional-political systems abroad, such as in the United States, (4) the social equalitarianism of the new lands, (5) religious and social utopianism, (6) gold fever — in Australia, South Africa, the United States, and Canada, (7) the propaganda of official governmental agencies, such as state and provincial immigration bureaus, (8) the promotional activities of railroads, such as the Northern Pacific, with agents in Europe, (9) the letters from immigrant-receiving countries enclosing remittances to help finance emigration of relatives and friends, and (10) the rapid establishment and spread of immigrant-American, immigrant-Argentinian, and other such immigrant communities which formed points of destination and constituted transitional havens enabling the emigrants to continue for a while in familiar patterns of life until the absorption into the new societies could be carried through, usually in a generation or two. These transitional cultures were highly useful and important in the acculturation process.

In the Far East, the central fact has been the enormous growth and concentration of population, with hundreds of millions of people crowded into areas incapable of maintaining life adequately, and, in times of famine, incapable of sustaining life at all. The fantastic population pressures in China, India, and other areas of southeast Asia such as Java and Malaya compel either large-scale emigration or the exploitation of new sources of food. Both in character and in volume, Far Eastern population movements have differed markedly from European. The principal population movements have been short-distance migrations from areas of heavy concentration to adjoining areas of less dense concentration, as from China into Manchuria. These have been movements of farmers, without capital, drifting in desperation toward seemingly greater opportunities. The second movement has been that of merchant classes from China into southeast Asia, into Malaya, Indonesia, and the island areas, and into the Philippines. From India there have been analogous migrations into Burma, Malaya, and Ceylon. A feature of the migrations to outlying regions has been contract labor or human merchandise. Emigration from Japan to continental Asia has been largely government promoted. Compared to the movement of peoples within the general Asian area, the emigration to the Americas and Europe has been very small indeed. Except for the short-distance migrants — chiefly farmers — the emigrants have been specialists of one kind or another, going to areas in which there is demand for such specialized services. This has been especially characteristic of the Chinese trading classes who have served from time immemorial as the middlemen of the Far East.[16] Indonesia with an enormous population of her own severely restricted immigration both during the Dutch era and since independence, and has undertaken to shift population from distressed areas to outlying, less populated areas.[17] The partition of India into East and West Pakistan and India brought one of the great population transfers in history when about 16 million people moved to new homes, much of the transfer being accomplished within one year's

[16] T. A. Silcock, "Migration Problems of the Far East," in Thomas, *Economics*, Chapter 18.

[17] Nathan Keyfitz, "Migration and the Economy of Indonesia," in Thomas, *Economics*, Chapter 19.

time. This event has been appropriately termed "the Great Displacement."[18]

Another significant population transfer in modern times has been that of Jews to Israel. As late as 1882 there were only 24,000 Jews in Palestine, but since then 1.5 million Jews have settled in Israel, and more are arriving every year. This population movement has been an exodus from countries of persecution to the refuge of a national homeland. Much of the world's Jewish population — which the Nazis reduced by 5.8 million — remains outside Israel, especially in the United States. Nevertheless, the ability of a small and economically unpromising area like Israel to absorb such a huge immigration within such a short period is a miracle and a monument to modern finance and technology.[19]

Since the huge transfer of Negroes from Africa during the fifteenth to the nineteenth centuries, there has been no significant emigration from Africa.

The positive contributions by immigrants to countries of immigration have been well described by a symposium held under the auspices of UNESCO and published by the latter in its Population and Culture Series in 1955 under the title *The Positive Contribution by Immigrants*.[20] It would be superfluous to try to add to this able volume.

That immigration has been a world phenomenon is a truism. That it will continue to be so seems doubtful. There are still underdeveloped areas in the world, such as the hinterlands of Brazil and Siberia, but the era of free movement of peoples is past and modern industrialism has so altered patterns of life as to make it improbable that there will be any large-scale agricultural migration, except under formal auspices and probably by force. The development of technology in countries of the Soviet bloc is having revolutionary results in the capacity of those countries to sustain large populations. In time, perhaps India, Indonesia, China, and other similarly overpopulated

[18] P. R. Brahmananda, "The Impact on India of Population Transfers in 1947 and After," in Thomas, *Economics*, Chapter 20.

[19] R. Bachi, "Immigration into Israel" in Thomas, *Economics*, Chapter 23.

[20] Paris: UNESCO, 1955.

countries can solve their pressing problems. The solutions will probably not be by the emigration of people, such as helped Italy to
relieve its distress, but from increase of productive capacity which
will, in turn, require industrialization.

We are therefore at the end of one era and in the beginnings of
another. It is appropriate that this volume of immigration studies
should be issued at such a time. It is a good time for inventory and
evaluation.

by HENRY A. POCHMANN

The Migration of Ideas

WE ASSUME that American culture (or civilization, if you prefer that term) results from the interplay or interaction between foreign influences and native conditioning — a foreign heritage and an American environment. That seems simple enough, but it doesn't help very much. In my own case, after studying these two factors for twenty-five years, and producing some ten or twelve pounds of letter-press on the subject of German-American relations — a quarter of a century during which hardly a day passed when I did not agonize over some question of what was *German* or *American* in the first place — I had finally to make this sober confession:

I have not found it possible anywhere precisely to define my terms, or even to distinguish between what might be termed *deutscher Geist* and American spirit, all formulations turning out to be so vague as to be meaningless, or so narrow as to be useless, or so comprehensive as to be self-contradictory.

I could only hope that the cumulative evidence which I piled up — of how a Kant inspired an Emerson to establish in Boston a *Prima Philosophia,* or how Goethe's *Faust* supplied motifs for Longfellow's *Golden Legend* — would speak for itself and be illuminating in both directions. Before I finally brought myself to make this chastening admission, I tried all kinds of palliatives, among them the idea that it is of first importance for the comparatist to remember (in the words of Howard Mumford Jones) that "what is borrowed, after all, is determined by what is wanted." But it soon occurred to me that not all importations are wanted. German critical transcendentalism was strenuously resisted as "The Latest Form of Infidelity," and German biblical criticism was condemned as the new Anti-Christ (whose name was David Strauss) over a hundred years ago, just as in our own day communism (though it stems neither originally nor exclusively from Russia) is fought by all means, fair and foul.

There is a difficulty that goes even deeper. It *may* be that what is borrowed is, in one way or another, wanted; but we can't very well discover what is wanted unless we know, first, what we have; and that is precisely what we don't know. If we knew, there would not have been the compelling urgency that some of us felt during the twenties to study foreign influences, for we had come to realize that unless we analyzed and assessed the many threads of foreign influence in our strangely and uniquely eclectic cultural fabric, our projected reinterpretation and critical rewriting of American literary history would soon come to a stuttering halt. Accordingly Howard Mumford Jones set to work to ascertain what is owing to French influence, Stanley Williams studied the Spanish impact, John Pritchard our classical heritage, I the Germanic, Theodore Blegen and his team (working from the historian's point of view) examined the Norwegian element, and others directed their efforts in still other directions — all in the hope that once the "foreign" strains were segregated, we should be left with a residue that we could call native, indigenous, or, if you like, "American."

Some of these undertakings have been completed; others are still in progress; one has been abandoned. Professor Jones, after publishing his pioneering work on French influence (up to 1848) and promising a second volume, announced in 1944: "I am unable to proceed to that mythical second volume because we still lack a comprehensive and illuminating history of ideas, of morals, and of taste in the United States."

It would seem that Mr. Jones and I stand at opposite poles — he the cautious conservative, I the intrepid adventurer. Now, Howard Jones has never been convicted of conservatism, and I am not known for enterprise. The truth is that Mr. Jones and I differ only about the time when it becomes profitable to make a beginning. I think we must make exploratory forays into uncharted areas, lest all investigations grind to a dead halt: the students of American culture stopped because they await the findings of the comparatists, while the latter wait for the former to complete their inquiries. There will be time enough for synthesis, *after* the reports of both sides are in. What is wanted at this stage, it seems to me, is not complication but simplification, not timidity but calculated risk — in short, individual investigators with a degree of courage and independence of critical judgment, even to the point of climbing pretty far out on the proverbial limb.

Whatever course is followed, there are, as I see it, three basic problems that confront us. These, if I may paraphrase Emerson, can be put in the form of three questions that we have a right and a duty to ask of ideas of whatever kind, wherever and whenever we encounter them. They are (1) What? (2) Whence? and (3) Whither?

The "What" of an immigrant idea involves problems of definition that I have already hinted at. If such an idea is an abstract one, it may be desperately hard to grasp, even by its tail. Fortunately, the history of ideas that concerns us is not, as Professor Jones has observed, "a bloodless dance of categories." For ideas are put to work; they contribute historical effects; what is difficult to determine is what makes an idea effective and when or how it becomes so. Surely Calvinism (or, if you like the larger term, Puritanism) was such an idea, or congeries of ideas, imported in the seventeenth century, which we can slice as thick or thin as we like. We can identify others that came later: the natural-rights theory (variously derived from Pufendorf to Locke), the Newtonian concept of order, the doctrine of perfectionism, Lockean sensationalism (with its far-reaching implications), Berkeleyan idealism, German transcendentalism, French eclecticism, realism, and naturalism, the social doctrines of Fourier, of Owen, and of Saint-Simon, mesmerism and phrenology, and, in our day, the new irrational psychology of Freud and Jung, sociopolitical theories like racism and communism, European techniques of writing from dadaism and surrealism to vorticism and existentialism, and the intellectualist criticism of the kind identified with the expatriates Ezra Pound and T. S. Eliot. The catalogue is endless.

But are we not to include also inventions, which start as ideas and influence other ideas? What about the railway, as a series of ideas from James Watt to George Stephenson, to the Union Pacific, to Walt Whitman's concept of one world as expressed in his poem *Passage to India*, or Wendell Willkie's adaptation of that idea? And what shall we do about Arkwright's idea of a cotton mill that wrought changes in the cultural pattern of our South (and our North) regarding which a factual history of the textile industry in the United States can tell us very little? Or, if railroads are too crass and cotton mills too pragmatic, what about methodologies? Shall we include, as I think we must, because of their far-reaching consequences, the seminar and laboratory methods of European universities and their concomitants, *Lehr- und Lern-freiheit*, that were adopted by and that re-made our own institutions? How far shall we go in tracing artistic techniques brought over by American artists sometime resident in Rome and Paris, or naturalistic and existentialist techniques of writing learned from Russian and French models? What ideas came over in immigrant chests, and what about superstitions and folkways? What about immigrant cohesiveness and exclusiveness, *deutsche Gemeinerei* and *Gemütlichkeit, Biergarten* and *smörgåsbord*, or Hänsel and Gretel, Baron von Münchausen, Saint Nicholas (or Santa Claus) and the Christmas tree, Hanukkah, Mardi Gras, and St. Patrick's Day? I need not go on.

The random instances I have cited could be made to illustrate how closely related are the questions What? and Whence?—i.e., how ideas come, who brought them, whom they influence, and how. In the case of Puritanism we are safe in asserting that it came over bodily as a full-blown theology from England (whatever its ultimate origins) in the minds of the first settlers of New England, though there were from the first notable differences in both theology and polity between Plymouth and Boston, Providence and Hartford. But how and by whom was such a basic Puritan tenet as congregationalism (i.e., the principle of self-determinism or autonomy in ecclesiastical policy) modified by later generations in ways to effect a complete reversal from the seventeenth-century Puritan's profession of his utter dependence on God to the doctrine of self-reliance voiced by his descendants in Emerson's day, by which time they declared that God is human and Man is divine? Was this change altogether owing to environmental influence, or did Puritanism carry within it the germ that wrought its own destruction, or did some catalyzing agents imported from abroad effect this doctrinal turnabout?

The mention of Emerson suggests New England transcendental-ism. Whence did it stem? Was it, as has been argued, inherent in Puritan idealism, or did it borrow also from German transcendental-ism, French eclecticism, Platonic idealism and neo-Platonic mysti-cism, and the Oriental scriptures to boot — and in what degrees and with what results for the several transcendentalists, each of whom had a Mission to attend to everybody else's business, so that they seldom agreed on anything more than to disagree among themselves *and* with everybody else? (As Lowell put it in *A Fable for Critics*: "I know they all went / For a general union of total dissent.") And what connections did the older transcendentalists have with the younger transcendentalists, the free religionists who espoused what they called the Religion of Humanity that certainly derived largely from Comte's positivism, as well as from the biblical criticism of the Tübingen school; or with the St. Louis Movement that was self-confessedly Hegelian in inspiration, despite its remarkably native character? None of the St. Louisans, save Brokmeyer, was foreign-born, and *he* came from Germany at an age when he had barely learned to read. He got his first indoctrination in Hegel through read-ing translated selections from Hegel's Introduction to his *Philosophy of History* in Frederic Henry Hedge's *Prose Writers of Germany*, one of the numerous books on German thought that issued from tran-scendentalist presses in New England. To be sure, he soon acquired Hegel's *Logic* and not only mastered it but translated it for his American-born associates and taught them to spin the "ever-spinning and interlacing triplets of Hegelian categories" until by their com-bined efforts they made available the entire corpus of Hegel in their native tongue and with it as their Bible, set forth to Hegelize the en-tire country. I have sketched, and only sketched, in a little book on the subject, how this unique phase of American idealism, starting in the East, moved west and then back again to come full circle at last and in the process (1) founded the Concord School of Philosophy, (2) organized, at the hands of William Torrey Harris, the United

States Bureau of Education on Hegelian principles, and (3) oriented or converted many, if not most, university departments of philosophy to Hegel, so that by the time I reached college there was hardly an institution of stature that did not have a full complement of courses from Leibnitz through Kant to Hegel and beyond.

Questions of Whence involve also the problem of where we shall look for our evidence of influence and acculturation. Historical and bibliographical data help, but much of our searching will have to be done among more elusive data. Theodore Dreiser's admitted adaptation of Haeckel's naturalism in *Sister Carrie* and of Nietzsche's amoralism in his "Trilogy of Desire" and the domestication of Freudian psychology in the plays of O'Neill and the novels of Sherwood Anderson cannot be evaluated with the precision with which the Battle of Gettysburg or an Act of Congress can be gauged. Their effect is not as dramatic as was the explosive shot of that embattled farmer's rifle, fired at Concord and heard round the world, or of the bomb hurled at Haymarket Square. Yet the vicarious aesthetic experiences of the novel-reader and the theatergoer are not less pervasively influential in shaping the American mind than is the actual participation of the soldier or of the anarchist in historically documented events; and that being so, they form an integral and legitimate part of the intellectual history of the United States.

I hurry on to my last question: Whither? That is, What for? To what purpose — good or bad? We are not ready to answer this kind of question, and may never be. But already there are rumblings of discontent with what is called the Hegelian strait jacket that Harris, as commissioner of education, attempted to fasten on the American public school system by departmentalizing and grading it into absolute Hegelian terms called units — fourteen to sixteen of which are still universally required of high school graduates; and there is talk, official and unofficial, in Washington and among regional accrediting agencies, among Deweyites and professional educationists, that Topsy has outgrown the garment that Harris fashioned for her. On the question of how salutary or pernicious foreign influences have been on writers like Longfellow, Lowell, and Holmes there is today spirited debate. It is noteworthy that Hawthorne, Melville, and

Thoreau representing the East and Mark Twain, Willa Cather, and Ole Rölvaag for the West are now rated as native writers and therefore in the Great American tradition, while Longfellow, Holmes, and Company are identified with the Genteel, the derivative, the European, or un-American tradition. Much of this kind of argument has not yet risen above the level of name-calling. The cosmopolitan party cites Dr. Johnson to the effect that patriotism is the last refuge of the scoundrel. The nativists declare that there is something basically wrong with all expatriates from Henry James to Ezra Pound. Finding life in America distasteful — it is alleged — they turned to Europe, but finding things no better there, they retreated within themselves, only to discover living with themselves equally impossible, so that there was nothing left for these now deracinated and desiccated Prufrocks but to lose themselves in the unintelligibility of a Pound or the waste land of an Eliot. Indeed, Pound is written off altogether as a committed Bedlamite, while Eliot, since he declared himself a conservative, a royalist, and a high-churchman, has willfully placed himself outside the Great Tradition; and from this point of view, both are good riddance. On the other side there are those whose very articulate defense of Pound and Eliot has about it the aura of a cult. It is among the prickly and thorny paths of these disparate opinions that the cultural historian fifty or a hundred years hence will have to pick his wary way.

And all this becomes doubly complicated because of the rapidity with which national and racial distinctions are disappearing. To illustrate, I would like to relate a story current at the University of Texas when I was a student. There was in Austin a venerable colored gem'man who was proud of having shaved every governor and every president of the university during all the years that he had operated his barber shop on Guadaloupe Street. One day, while working on Robert Vinson, then president of the university, he said: "Mistah Vinson, ef'n I wuz daid, you'd be sorry, wouldn't you, sah?" Mr. Vinson said he would be. "An' you'd send flowers, wouldn't you?" Mr. Vinson allowed he would. "Den, sah," said Jim, "ef'n I could have my d'ruthers, I'd ruther have de money while I'se alive." Mr. Vinson took the hint, and so did many of Jim's other friends, and raised a sum sufficient to send Jim's boy to the Prairie View Normal College for Negroes and Jim on a tour of the United States, with New England as his easternmost destination. Some time after Jim's departure, President Vinson was delighted to receive a gaudy picture postcard of Plymouth Rock, postmarked Plymouth, Mass., and bearing this message: "Dear Mr. Vinson, *this* is where our ancestors landed!"

by FRANKLIN D. SCOTT

The Immigration Theme
in the Framework of National Groups

THE process of migration to America is primarily an individual phenomenon. In his decision to emigrate, in the circumstances of his travel, in the problems of his resettlement, each person is different from every other person, just as his thumbprints are a peculiar and individual pattern. For the ideal and thorough study of immigration to the United States we should therefore have some 39 million biographies, buttressed with intelligence tests, letters of recommendation, lie detector tests, and psychiatric reports. Then we could make scientific classifications and analyses, and with a battery of IBM machines run by an army of researchers we might have some data compiled by the year 3000. Lacking such information and/or the time to digest it, we must choose some ready-made classifications — for even individuals (like thumbprints) can be grouped into broad categories — and sample, as best we can, the cases within them. Then we find ourselves thwarted, of course, by distortions in the sample, since we are largely limited to the records of immigrants who happened to be literate — and who wanted to write.

Theodore C. Blegen, for example, was not only industrious and foresighted; he had, in the Norwegians with whom he worked and whose history he compiled, an extraordinarily literate group of people, and it is they as well as he who have created the magnificent five-foot shelf of books of the Norwegian-American Historical Association.

Even if not all national groups were so literarily inclined, could we find, in the search for some workable scheme of breaking up the mass into significant units, any more significant unit than the nation in Europe and the national group in the United States?

Other groupings are of course possible. Time units have some meaning, especially for the development of America. But the fact that such and such a number of immigrants arrived in 1630 or in 1851, or even in a certain decade or century, tells but a small portion of the story. Diversities are great and unifying factors meager. That a certain proportion of these immigrants belonged to a lower or a higher economic stratum, or a certain sex or age, or professed a certain religious belief, or had attained a known level of education — all such factors help to delineate the nature of the immigrant a bit more clearly. But the characteristic that was probably the most significant of all, and probably the most tenacious, was nationality. Fortunately this is also one of the characteristics most readily identified.

To be impressed with the importance of nationality one need only ask himself how different might American culture have become had the Spanish instead of the British settled the eastern seaboard — or the French, or the Russians? Or think of the different flavor of life today in communities of different national background — such as New Orleans and Milwaukee, or Santa Fe and Boston.

Charles A. Beard once said that the history of the Middle West, particularly, must be written as the history of its immigrant national groups; and that each must do its own writing because each possessed the language and cultural understanding which an outsider could not get. The Norwegians, the Swedes, and the Danes could do it; Germans, he thought, were too much interested in drinking beer together; Poles might, for they had an occasional scholar; the Italians among the immigrants were laborers and lacked scholars.[1] Despite exaggeration and oversimplification Beard was doubtless largely correct. Yet there are inherent dangers in letting the sons or grandsons of a country be the only ones to write the history of their national groups. On the one hand filiopietism is not dead. On the other hand languages and cultures *can* be learned by outsiders, and not only

[1] As told to Mr. Vilas Johnson in conversation.

greater impartiality but possibly an improved perspective attained thereby. Why not let a Russian-American study the Italian-Americans, for example, and a French-American study the Polish-Americans?

But is the national group a practicable and fruitful unit for study? Will it give us the kind of answers we want? Not in all cases, of course, but let us examine briefly four of the major areas of study and see what can be done with the national groups in those areas: (1) the causes of emigration from Europe; (2) the character of the migrating people; (3) the effect of emigration on the country of origin; and (4) the adaptation to America.

If our purpose is to seek for the causes of emigration from Europe, will the national approach be useful? The answer must surely be Yes. Disregarding for the moment the question of the "pull of America," which is the other side of the shield, did not the fundamental causes for emigration lie within the separate national communities of Europe? And were they not, therefore, inevitably different for different nations? Was it not factors deep-rooted in their national societies that caused Irish and Norwegians to migrate in larger numbers than other groups? Was it not also national factors that brought, at a later period, the immense movement of Poles and Italians? The factors were not necessarily the same or even analogous, but they were in all cases conditions rooted in national life, and often affected by the laws of national states. For example, the Norwegian of the nineteenth century was perhaps seeking above all *land*, which was pathetically scarce at home where only 3 per cent of the total was arable; the Italian of the twentieth century (to a large extent) was not so much seeking land as money to take back home, or a life in the city. The British, according to Rowland Berthoff,[2] were skilled or semiskilled craftsmen more than were the emigrants from other countries, and came expecting jobs similar to those they had held at home. Migration was affected by national economic problems, taxation, required military service; and also by the national social structure, church

---

[2] *British Immigrants in Industrial America, 1790–1950* (Cambridge, Mass.: Harvard University Press, 1953).

policy, land distribution, population pressures — a whole host of factors that were associated with particular states and societies much more than with Europe as a whole or the world. Even recruitment of immigrants by the direct appeals of steamship agencies, or through the personal "America letters" sent home by relatives and friends who had made the great trek, tended to be national in scope, partly for the very good reason of language. Since the time of Sir Walter Raleigh and Benjamin Franklin and the Marquis de Lafayette and scores of others who captured the popular imagination, Europeans had created for themselves a "myth of America," often making in their minds this half-known land across the seas into everything they most lacked but wanted in their own earth-bound existence. The myth of the noble red man is but a part of this larger image, an image that took differing shapes in accord with the oppressions and the hopes of men of various nations. The myth of America is a phenomenon requiring intensive study by men of insight, who understand that people act not on the basis of reality but on what they think and feel.

As for the multifarious individual causes that determined O'Reilly and Olson and Smelnitsky and Neapolis to leave oppressive security for dangerous uncertainty, it is obvious that they were more closely connected with the national and local scene than with any general European ferment.

In this whole area of nation-related causes of emigration an impressive amount of work has been done. But to a large extent this research has been confined to study of *particular* national backgrounds. While more case studies are needed in this same area, it is time someone set his sights on the wider goal of comparative studies — using the national studies, shaping their findings into relatable if not parallel items, and comparing the underlying forces of emigration in different countries and at different times.[3] Extension of this

[3] A good introduction to the history and problems of this subject is Maurice R. Davie, *World Immigration* (New York: Macmillan, 1936). In a paper prepared for the XI International Congress of Historical Sciences, Stockholm 1960, Frank Thistlethwaite provides an excellent and stimulating survey of work done in the whole field of emigration-immigration studies (*Rapports* (Stockholm: Almqvist and Wiksell, 1960), V, 32–60). See also Franklin D. Scott, "The Study of the Effect of Emigration," to be published in *Scandinavian Economic History*, 1961.

comparative approach to encompass all the immigrant-receiving countries, such as Australia, Canada, South Africa, Brazil, Argentina, would enrich our understanding of the process of migration, and would throw some welcome perspective on the migration to the United States (which was the largest but by no means the sole movement); it would be interesting to know why some people did *not* come to the United States, and why they came in different proportions from different countries. The techniques of all the social sciences — history, psychology, sociology, plus economics and geography and government — must be mobilized for this kind of approach. Here is a vast subject to be dealt with, and it should be dealt with as a whole, not split up into disciplinary segments. The next breakthrough in synthesis and understanding of why men migrate may well come in this trans-disciplinary, trans-national, comparative realm.

When we turn to a second topic such as the character of the migratory horde, we have, perhaps, better data than on any other phase of the migration. Census reports, ship manifests, parish registers in the old country, give us a fairly accurate record of numbers by age and sex, of the time of their migration, of geographic point of origin, and even of class and occupational status. Here again there is a place for comparative studies between countries as to the reasons for the varying proportions of rural and urban emigrants, for the greater proportions from some countries than from others of educated persons and of men with money. Such investigations might show us much both about the emigrating classes and also about social conditions and opportunities in various lands. More careful study of the periodization of emigrant movements as related to revolutions and social reform is certainly necessary. Only recently, for example, has the myth been exploded that the swelling German migration of the 1850's was largely made up of liberals disappointed with the failure of the Revolution of 1848.[4]

[4] But the myths that we want to believe die hard, and the picture of persecuted liberals fleeing European oppression for the freedom and brotherhood of America is dear to American hearts. Furthermore, there is some truth in the idea, and Carl Schurz to prove it. But there are also many instances where it has no relevance. For the German migration of 1848–55 Marcus L. Hansen showed that the typical

We would be greatly enlightened if we could learn more about the psychological makeup of the emigrants as individuals. To what extent were they the perpetually discontented, unable to adjust to any society? The restless rootlessness of many who continued to wander instead of settling indicates that this may be an important characteristic. Perhaps it is only remotely related to national origin, yet these were all people who in the first instance had failed — or been condemned to failure — in their adaptation to their native community. Being unable to adjust to or manipulate their own society they could and did attempt to build a new society in a new environment. They were at the very least men and women able to make decisions and to act, but undoubtedly many of them were inherent nonconformists. Migration gave such people a major opportunity to make a choice. But how much were the migrants the daring adventurers, the men of inventive mind, leaving behind them the men of little faith and the lovers of stability?[5]

Whatever may be the answer to the last question, a third topic for rewarding study by way of the national group concerns the effect of emigration on the country of origin. To examine this for Europe as a whole is a problem too vast, complex, unrealistic. At the other extreme, on the local level one can find towns decimated in population, with homes and farms abandoned; others where life has been changed by money sent back to the village from emigrants become millionaires. But such phenomena are special, atypical. Again the national unit is the largest one that is possible and the smallest one that is significant.[6]

emigrant was a small-holder driven out by a combination of bad harvests and the difficult shift to a money economy — ironically partly a result of the *success* of 1848 reforms; 97 out of every 100 emigrants were from "Germany west of the Elbe" ("The Revolution of 1848 and German Emigration," *Journal of Economic and Business History*, 2:630–58 (August 1930)).

[5] Olof Thörn in Sweden has unearthed the correspondence files of a group of emigrant agents active in Sweden in the 1880's, and the letters in this find give some insights into the minds and purposes of the emigrants. Two preliminary articles based on these materials are published in the *Swedish Pioneer Historical Quarterly*, 10:3–24 (January 1959) and 10:52–66 (April 1959).

[6] Occasionally of course regions such as Scotland, southern Italy, parts of Germany, and the Ukraine may be significant in themselves and also possess statistics

Emigration is of course but one of the many influences producing change; it is impossible to isolate it completely from other forces such as industrialization, urbanization, new transportation routes, student travel, and tourism. But such differentiations must be attempted. Perhaps a little can be done to trace where and how some of the remittance money was spent — here at least is something tangible. Here is required a comparison technique within the national culture, as well as between countries, and a willingness to weigh imponderables, to deal with reasoned probabilities rather than with mathematical certainties. No one can doubt that the departure of hundreds of thousands of young men and women had real impact on many a small country — and no one has yet found a way to measure this effect satisfactorily. Perhaps the effect was more indirect than direct, as in Sweden where the exodus produced a major parliament-sponsored social inquiry, which inquiry in turn produced (or at least helped to produce) a sweeping program of social legislation. Perhaps the effect was largely in that spirit of change that pervaded the atmosphere in the new America and that spread like a contagion among the lowlier people of the Old World. What did emigration have to do with the enhancement throughout the world of the impetus toward progress, self-improvement? [7]

In still broader terms, to find the effect of the Great Migration

that can be isolated; the statistical problem is one of the major hurdles in dealing with sub-national groups.

[7] An increasing number of studies, both articles and books, deal with cultural interchange, but seldom does anyone attempt to distinguish between emigration and the other forces at work. The pioneering study of William I. Thomas and Florian Znaniecki, *The Polish Peasant in Europe and America* (Vols. I, II, Chicago: University of Chicago Press, 1918; Vols. III, IV, V, Boston: Badger, 1919–20), has not been followed by really parallel research for other groups. Later volumes that deal with this topic among others in a broader setting include Halvdan Koht, *The American Spirit in Europe* (Philadelphia: University of Pennsylvania Press, 1949); Michael Kraus, *The Atlantic Civilization: Eighteenth Century Origins* (Ithaca, N.Y.: Cornell University Press, 1949); Theodore Saloutos, *They Remember America: The Story of the Repatriated Greek-Americans* (Berkeley and Los Angeles: University of California Press, 1956); and Arnold Schrier, *Ireland and the American Emigration, 1850–1900* (Minneapolis: University of Minnesota Press, 1958). Among the best of the source materials is Gustav Sundbärg's mine of information in the twenty-one volumes of reports and analyses of Swedish emigration known as *Emigrationsutredningen* (Stockholm: Norstedt, 1908–13).

one must reckon with the creation and expansion of the United States and its impact on peoples and economies the world over, for it is immigration, primarily from Europe, that has made the United States (and Canada, South Africa, Australia, etc.). Without immigration this great power would not exist. This is a subject that must be treated in a different frame of reference, but it is a matter of overwhelming importance, and inseparable from migration.

On just the first part of the subject, however — the influence of the departing thousands, economically, politically, socially, psychologically, on their nation's culture — we have a challenging field of investigation. Here bold spirits are required with their hypotheses, and also careful and painstaking researchers to confirm and to destroy hypotheses. Results of investigation along this line may in the course of time help to explain how societies change, why some progress dramatically, why others stagnate and decay.

A fourth facet of this national emphasis would focus on the United States. It would study the national-group communities in this country, in urban and rural areas, perhaps with the historical-sociological techniques developed by Merle Curti[8] and the historical-folkloristic methods used by Richard Dorson.[9] What did immigrants carry with them in the way of persistent ideas and attitudes, folklore, values? As they came to the New World and launched new projects were they acting from innate personal impulses or were they rather responding to the challenges newly discovered on the frontier?

Why were peoples from many different countries more religious in the United States than were their compatriots at home — was it because the minister enjoyed greater prestige and authority in a milieu in which the newcomers were a puzzled minority, or was it because of the need among these people for the close social ties that a church could bring? Or was it because the church with its familiar ritual and language seemed a means of maintaining the ties with home?

[8] *The Making of an American Community: A Case Study of Democracy in a Frontier County* (Stanford, Calif.: Stanford University Press, 1959). This is a thorough study of Trempealeau County, Wisconsin.

[9] The latest in a series of works by Dorson is *American Folklore* (Chicago: University of Chicago Press, 1959).

The immigrant's need for associating with his fellow-nationals is undoubtedly enhanced by his loneliness in America. When the informal associations of inherited neighborhood have broken down he has to formalize his friendships. The tendency to join national lodges and singing societies and clubs of all kinds may seem only natural in the civilization of the organization man, but if the efflorescence of such associations among immigrants is abnormally high it calls for some psychological analysis. And why do certain nationalities become absorbed more quickly and fully than others into the American scene — or do they?

As a figure of speech "the melting pot" probably makes us all a bit uncomfortable because of its palpable exaggeration. The process of amalgamation maybe should instead be called the salad bowl. For a piece of lettuce, even after soaking in French dressing, is still a piece of lettuce. Immigrants retained the characteristics bred into them as children, and probably most of them retained a strong though confused sense of attachment to the motherland.[10] A few immigrants who plan definitely to return to the old country may live in the new land for years and never become a part of it. They wear their indigenous culture as a protective cloak; they live in little extra-territorial enclaves of their own personalities until they can buy their tickets home and settle down once more in the surroundings of their childhood. Any who return, as a result of previous planning or unforeseen circumstance, may after going "home" face disillusionment in a society that has changed in their absence, and they may at last realize that in the attempt to hold fast to their inheritance they have ended by losing not one world but two.[11]

[10] In a chapter on "The Fabric of Society" Bessie Louise Pierce, in her *History of Chicago*, Vol. III (New York: Knopf, 1957), provides an excellent brief survey of the many immigrant groups of the city in the period 1871–93, while they struggled through the transition from loyalties to the old country to full acceptance of the new.

[11] One who expressed this feeling in poignant phrase in his memoirs was Gustaf Unonius, who returned to Sweden after seventeen years in America, much of that time spent as an Episcopal minister to a Swedish-Norwegian flock in Chicago: "We, too — though we could not but admit that the country where we had spent so many years had, at least for us, many advantages over the country we had left — still we 'longed for our mother's hut.' In reality — we knew that well — there was

To what extent did immigrants arriving in the United States seek the kind of work for which they had been trained at home? As already indicated, Berthoff found that the British were significantly different in this respect from the "broad, undifferentiated stream" of Continental emigrants; more were skilled or semiskilled craftsmen, fewer were peasants. Among coal miners in the United States 88 per cent of the Scotch and Welsh and 83 per cent of the English, but only 55 per cent of the Germans, had been miners before emigration. In copper mining 60 per cent of the English had been miners at home, but only 18 per cent of the Swedes and 13 per cent of the Germans. In iron mining the proportions were 54 per cent for the English, 10 per cent for the Swedes, and 15 per cent for the north Italians.[12] Are such differences the result of national conditions abroad, or are they due to special opportunities for English-trained and English-speaking personnel in America? In general, do emigrants seek the same kind of work they have done before, or do they want something quite different? Certainly the Irish immigrants had not had much experience as policemen or politicians in the Emerald Isle — was it long-thwarted urges that drew them into these activities in American cities? And why, on the other hand, were the frustrated farmers of barren and resisting rock in Norway and Sweden drawn by the thousands to the black soil of the midwestern prairies? In the pluralistic, heterogeneous society of America does the immigrant really become more tolerant of racial diversity? Why was the upper Mississippi valley, with a heavy concentration of immigrants from northern Europe, the most "isolationist" section of the country? What part does the foreign-language press play in the processes of Americaniza-

no longer such a place awaiting us. But our fatherland was 'our mother's hut,' and thither we were driven by our longing, without realizing that it might no longer have a place for those who had once despised its poverty and might now come to stand like strangers at its threshold. . . . among my numerous missteps in life there are especially two for which I may properly blame myself: one, that I ever emigrated to America; the other, that after I had made my home and found my field of service there, I returned from that country." (*A Pioneer in Northwest America, 1841– 1858: The Memoirs of Gustaf Unonius*, Vol. II, translated by Jonas O. Backlund and edited by Nils W. Olsson (Minneapolis: Published for the Swedish Pioneer Historical Society by the University of Minnesota Press, 1960), pp. 320, 322.)

[12] Berthoff, *British Immigrants in Industrial America*, pp. 21–29.

tion (or of retention of the old language and habits)? And here again one needs not only studies of particular national newspapers, such as have been successfully made,[13] but comparative studies of the press in different languages — a thing difficult, of course, because of the diverse languages involved.

Hosts of questions arise, centering again and again around the national group. Are we not failing to study sufficiently in depth, before persons and materials vanish, the major human phenomenon of United States history — if not of world history? Just as the geographic frontier closed in 1890, so the immigration frontier closed about 1920. The nations now have to seek new solutions for the "population explosion."

A major interdisciplinary, organized effort ought to be made, to tap the informational materials — both people and documents — throughout the United States which can still throw light on this closed chapter of American history. In any such effort the national groups must be the indispensable allies of the scholars.

[13] One example of this type of study is Arlow Andersen, *The Immigrant Takes His Stand. The Norwegian-American Press and Public Affairs, 1847–1872* (Northfield, Minn.: Norwegian-American Historical Association, 1953).

by CARLTON C. QUALEY

Prospects for Materials in Immigration Studies

AT FIRST glance the materials for a history of American immigration seem voluminous, but closer inspection reveals that they are in fact inadequate. Happily there are large reservoirs of materials still to be tapped, and it is the purpose of this paper to indicate what these are and how they may be exploited for further study, and for ultimate synthesis.

Oddly enough there is no adequate comprehensive bibliography of the history of immigration. The most recent — that published by the George Washington University in 1956 — is incomplete, somewhat hastily compiled, and, as is the fate of all bibliographies, already out of date.[1] The student interested in the whole range of immigration history will find it necessary to search through innumerable monographs and the sprawling publications of immigrant-group organizations. Three of these may be cited as illustrations: the *Bibliography of German Culture in America to 1940*, compiled and edited by Henry A. Pochmann and Arthur R. Schultz;[2] O. Fritiof Ander's reference list for Swedish immigration; and the annual listing of publications in Norwegian-American history included in *Norwegian-American Studies and Records*.[3]

[1] *A Report on World Population Migrations as Related to the United States of America* (Washington, D.C.: George Washington University, 1956).

[2] Madison, Wis.: University of Wisconsin Press, 1953.

[3] Ander, *The Cultural Heritage of the Swedish Immigrant. Selected References* (Rock Island, Ill.: Augustana College Library, 1956); *Norwegian-American Studies and Records*, 20 vols. to date (Northfield, Minn.: Norwegian-American Historical Association, 1926–59).

Nor will the student find bibliographical searches in the principal depositories of immigration materials wholly satisfactory, for in many places the materials have not been properly organized and indexed. The New York Public Library not only is the most useful depository of immigration materials generally, but has also done more than any other institution to make its vast collection of materials readily available to the scholar. Other depositories of varying richness of resources and usefulness are the Harvard University Libraries (especially the Marcus L. Hansen papers), the Library of Congress, the National Archives, the state historical societies of Wisconsin and Minnesota, and the archives of the Church of the Latter-day Saints in Salt Lake City. Although it would be convenient to establish a central depository of immigration materials, such a plan is not feasible. It is, however, entirely feasible to undertake the compilation of a general bibliography adequate as a working tool for students of immigration.

In what is clearly the primary resource field the student is gratified by a distinct improvement in United States statistics, thanks to the recent publications in the Census Monograph Series sponsored by the Social Science Research Council and the Bureau of the Census.[4] Despite more adequate statistical studies of United States censuses, however, much valuable material still remains buried in the manuscript census schedules, particularly those before the census of 1880, which was the first to give information on the birthplace of parents and thus provide a more nearly adequate indication of population stocks. Except for fire damage to some of these records, they are open for use up through the census of 1910 which — under the fifty-year rule — has just become available to scholars. Anyone who has worked in the manuscript census schedules of the United States knows how rich is the information buried there, but in view of the formidable amount of time and energy required to excavate this information we can expect only fragmentary work in these materials for some time to come.

[4] E. P. Hutchinson, *Immigrants and Their Children, 1850–1950* (New York: Wiley, 1956); Conrad and Irene B. Taeuber, *The Changing Population of the United States* (New York: Wiley, 1958).

While American statistics are far from satisfactory, those of European nations are even less adequate, and this despite the work of agencies of the League of Nations and the United Nations. The admirable study of British emigration statistics in Brinley Thomas's *Migration and Economic Growth* deserves extensive imitation elsewhere.[5] European governments were frequently both perfunctory and inaccurate in keeping their emigration statistics, but a comparative study of European and American statistics is sometimes satisfactory and often illuminating.

Among the richest resources for the historian of immigration are the "America letters" written by emigrants back to their relatives and friends, or to the newspapers. In this field Theodore Blegen has been a pioneer, and the monument to his energy and zeal is the exciting collection of Norwegian emigrant letters called *Land of Their Choice*.[6] Would that we had a shelf of such volumes representing all emigrant groups! A few other collections of such letters have been published,[7] but there is no general collection of America letters despite several attempts to organize support for such a project. Scholars should renew their efforts to collect and publish, or microfilm, these invaluable — and rapidly vanishing — materials. The number available is determined in varying measure by the literacy of the respective emigrant groups, the interest in emigration displayed by homeland newspapers, and the conscientiousness of governmental and historical agencies in collecting and servicing these letters. Enough should be available to fill a score or more volumes.

Despite extensive use of newspapers by students of individual immigrant groups, especially the Norwegian, Swedish, German, English, and Irish, the newspaper files of the countries of emigration and of the American immigrant press constitute a tremendous resource which has as yet scarcely been mined. There are two major obstacles to their general exploitation: one is the physical problem of access

[5] Cambridge, Eng.: Cambridge University Press, 1954.

[6] Minneapolis: University of Minnesota Press, 1955.

[7] Such as Henry S. Lucas, ed., *Dutch Immigrant Memoirs and Related Writings* (2 vols.; Assen, Netherlands: Van Gorcum, 1955), and Alan Conway, ed., *The Welsh in America: Letters from the Immigrants* (Minneapolis: University of Minnesota Press, 1961).

to the files, the second is language. As to the first, no one person can hope to level this mountainous file of papers. What is needed is a sustained cooperative effort, with extensive use of microfilming. Obviously such a task force will need to include workers who command a great variety of languages. As American students are notoriously monolingual, this work must enlist the nationals of various countries of emigration. Only in this way can we hope to solve the problem of language.

The governmental archives of the United States and of foreign countries are filled with unexploited materials. The consular reports — especially for periods of special concern about immigration — contain useful data, often of a specialized nature such as those on the extent of pauperism. The files of immigration bureaus, port authorities, and health agencies, federal and state court records, and the legislative records of all governments contain material that would be helpful to the historian. There have been periodic official investigations of emigration and immigration, both in the United States and in European states. In the field of governmental records we encounter special problems in this era of the cold war. While the normal difficulties in the use of governmental records remain for western European states, these difficulties are magnified and multiplied when one attempts to get at records of nations in eastern Europe. For example, all the materials relating to Russian emigration are stored in the Ministry of Foreign Affairs in Moscow, and access to them involves an elaborate procedure. Few Americans, in fact, have been permitted to work in Russian archives. There is some hope of increased exchange of microfilmed material, but the progress is limited. Perhaps under the auspices of organizations of archivists and historians all countries can gradually be persuaded to open their archives to use by scholars.

The pioneer study of immigrant acculturation in the United States is Thomas and Znaniecki's *Polish Peasant in Europe and America*, now over forty years old; two recent volumes reveal the wealth of materials readily available to the researcher: Oscar Handlin's *Boston's Immigrants*,[8] newly revised, and a model study of the reaction

[8] Cambridge, Mass.: Harvard University Press, 1959.

[129]

of a community to its immigrants, and Robert Ernst's *Immigrant Life in New York City, 1825–63*.[9] To list other monographic studies would stray from the primary purpose of this paper, but those cited may serve as examples of what should be done for other American cities, communities, and immigrant groups. For rural areas the recent collaborative study of Trempealeau County, Wisconsin, directed by Professor Merle Curti, should prove instructive.[10]

Business archives contain as yet unexploited materials, as we can see in Charlotte Erickson's *American Industry and the European Immigrant, 1860–1885*.[11] It is to be hoped that this study of immigrant recruiting will be followed by others covering all areas of Europe. Another type of investigation into unexploited materials is the study of the emigrant traffic out of Bremen by Ludwig Beutin.[12] Aside from these there are no careful studies of the great emigrant ports of Europe, nor have scholars concerned themselves with the history of remittances from emigrants to homeland relatives and friends.[13] Since these remittances run into millions upon millions of dollars, since a considerable part of late nineteenth- and early twentieth-century emigration was financed by remittances, and since the remittances had important effects on European economies, a livelier attention to this subject would seem justified.

In addition, it should be noted that another very important body of materials concerning economic aspects of immigration is to be found in the railroad archives, such as those in the Newberry Library in Chicago and in other depositories, notably the headquarters of the railroads themselves. To the older studies by Hedges, Gates, and Overton will be added others now in preparation, and it is to be hoped that eventually the immigration activities of all our railroads,

[9] New York: King's Crown Press, 1949.

[10] *The Making of an American Community: A Case Study of Democracy in a Frontier County* (Stanford, Calif.: Stanford University Press, 1959).

[11] Cambridge, Mass.: Harvard University Press, 1957.

[12] *Bremen und Amerika. Zur Geschichte der Weltwirtschaft und der Beziehungen Deutschlands zu den Vereinigten Staaten* (Bremen: C. Schünemann, 1953).

[13] See Franklin D. Scott, "The Causes and Consequences of Emigration from Sweden" in *Chronicle* (Philadelphia, American Swedish Historical Foundation), Spring 1955; Arnold Schrier, *Ireland and the American Emigration, 1850–1900* (Minneapolis: University of Minnesota Press, 1958), Chapter 6.

and of foreign railroads as well, will be studied and reported.[14] No less urgent is the need for adequate histories of the great transatlantic shipping companies which profited so largely from human freight.

It is the emigration and immigration of the peoples of western Europe that has been most thoroughly investigated. Yet even the familiar story of Norwegian, Swedish, Dutch, English, Irish, German, Jewish, and Italian immigration is still but incompletely recorded.[15] And, despite a good many capital articles and some brief volumes, we still have no adequate histories of emigration from Denmark, Finland, Iceland, Scotland, Belgium, France, Switzerland, Spain, and Portugal — truly a formidable list!

As we move eastward in Europe, the gaps in the literature of emigration become startlingly obvious. In addition to the significant early

[14] J. B. Hedges, *Henry Villard and the Railways of the Northwest* (New Haven: Yale University Press, 1930); Paul W. Gates, *The Illinois Central Railroad and Its Colonization Work* (Cambridge, Mass.: Harvard University Press, 1934); Richard Overton, *Burlington West* (Cambridge, Mass.: Harvard University Press, 1941).

[15] Theodore C. Blegen, *Norwegian Migration to America* (2 vols.; Northfield, Minn.: Norwegian-American Historical Association, 1931, 1940); Carlton C. Qualey, *Norwegian Settlement in the United States* (Northfield, Minn.: Norwegian-American Historical Association, 1938); Kenneth O. Bjork, *West of the Great Divide: Norwegian Migration to the Pacific Coast, 1847–1893* (Northfield, Minn.: Norwegian-American Historical Association, 1958); George M. Stephenson, *The Religious Aspects of Swedish Immigration* (Minneapolis: University of Minnesota Press, 1932); Florence E. Janson, *The Background of Swedish Immigration, 1840–1930* (Chicago: University of Chicago Press, 1931); Henry S. Lucas, *Netherlanders in America: Dutch Immigration to the United States and Canada, 1789–1950* (Ann Arbor: University of Michigan Press, 1955); Rowland T. Berthoff, *British Immigrants in Industrial America, 1790–1950* (Cambridge, Mass.: Harvard University Press, 1953); Wilbur S. Shepperson, *British Emigration to North America: Projects and Opinions in the Early Victorian Period* (Oxford: Blackwell; Minneapolis: University of Minnesota Press, 1957); Carl Wittke, *The Irish in America* (Baton Rouge: Louisiana State University Press, 1956); William F. Adams, *Ireland and Irish Emigration to the New World from 1815 to the Famine* (New Haven: Yale University Press, 1932); Schrier, *Ireland and the American Emigration*; John A. Hawgood, *The Tragedy of German-America* (New York: Putnam, 1940); Henry A. Pochmann, *German Culture in America: Philosophical and Literary Influences, 1600–1900* (Madison: University of Wisconsin Press, 1957); Rufus Learsi, *The Jews in America: A History* (Cleveland and New York: World, 1954); Oscar Handlin, *Adventure in Freedom: Three Hundred Years of Jewish Life in America* (New York: McGraw-Hill, 1954); Robert F. Foerster, *The Italian Emigration of Our Times*, Harvard Economic Studies, no. 20 (Cambridge, Mass.: Harvard University Press, 1919). Obviously these references do not exhaust the bibliography for each of the national groups, but they are perhaps the representative volumes.

work of Thomas and Znaniecki on the Poles, a work primarily socio-logical, we need a full study of Polish immigration to America.[16] Nor have we any studies of consequence on the coming of the peoples of the Baltic states. Russian emigration still awaits its historian: it may prove a long wait! There have been some attempts to record emigration by the central European peoples — Austrians, Hungar-ians, Bohemians, Moravians, Ruthenians, and others, but none of these is adequate. Nor is the situation for the southern Slav peoples any better.[17] Nor do we have histories of any consequence concern-ing emigration of any of the Middle Eastern peoples, Turks, Iraqi, Iranians, Arabs, and others, nor any studies of African population movements to the United States since the days of slavery.

Although some studies of Asiatic emigration were made during the period of the immigration restriction controversy, we still lack adequate histories of Chinese, Japanese, and other Far Eastern emi-gration. Indeed this vast field of investigation is untouched. Surpris-ingly enough, much the same can be said of immigration from the many nations south of the Rio Grande. Canadian immigration has been recorded with learning and insight,[18] and Mexican immigration has not been wholly neglected.[19]

There is little doubt that rising interest in the impact of the United States on the rest of the world will have some consequences for the history of immigration. There have been but few studies of value in this area,[20] and it is to be hoped that European historians will make contributions to this strangely neglected chapter of European history.

[16] William I. Thomas and Florian Znaniecki, *The Polish Peasant in Europe and America* (2 vols., 2nd edition; New York: Knopf, 1927).

[17] It is to be hoped that the recent study by Theodore Saloutos, *They Remember America: The Story of the Repatriated Greek-Americans* (Berkeley and Los An-geles: University of California Press, 1956) will be followed by a full account of Greek immigration.

[18] Marcus L. Hansen and John B. Brebner, *The Mingling of the Canadian and American Peoples* (New Haven: Yale University Press, 1940).

[19] Manuel Gamio, *Mexican Immigration to the United States* (Chicago: Univer-sity of Chicago Press, 1930).

[20] Such as Richard H. Heindel, *The American Impact on Great Britain, 1898–1914* (Philadelphia: University of Pennsylvania Press, 1940); Louis L. Gerson, *Woodrow Wilson and the Rebirth of Poland, 1914–1920* (New Haven: Yale Univer-sity Press, 1953); Schrier, *Ireland and the American Emigration.*

Enough has been said to indicate that we have a long way to go before we have adequately surveyed and tilled the rich field of emigration and immigration. Much of this field work will have to be carried on in university seminars. Regrettably few seminars have been, or are, devoted exclusively to immigration: notable exceptions are those which were directed by the late Professor George M. Stephenson and by Dean Theodore C. Blegen at the University of Minnesota, and by Professor Oscar Handlin at Harvard University. There is at this writing no graduate seminar devoted exclusively to study of immigration at a major American university. There are, of course, distinguished scholars who have inspired and guided doctoral studies in this field: Marcus L. Hansen at the University of Illinois, Carl Wittke at Western Reserve University, Franklin Scott at Northwestern University, Merle Curti at the University of Wisconsin, Paul Gates at Cornell University, Arthur M. Schlesinger, Sr., at Harvard University, and Allan Nevins at Columbia University, among others. Because immigration is not formally studied in seminars or even in courses at most universities, students come to the field more or less by chance. This situation is understandable but none the less regrettable. Perhaps this volume can stimulate greater activity in the promotion of studies of population movements and their consequences. Only after scholars have completed a substantial number of monographic studies can we hope to write that full-dress history of American immigration essential to our understanding of American and of world history.

by COLMAN J. BARRY, O.S.B.

New Prospects in Immigration Studies

Every historian in this field doubtless has his own ideas and plans for the future development of subjects and areas of immigration studies. One of the distinctive satisfactions of history is this revising of one's conclusions, allowing the changing shapes and colors of new research to permit discovery of something new. And I am certain that others have more valuable insights into the possibilities of immigration studies than I. I should like, however, to suggest some considerations which might stimulate a broader understanding of this topic while relating the parts to the whole.

The approaching Lincoln-Civil War centennial, with its flood of research already threatening to inundate us, could provide opportunities for more of the larger perspective we all desire. For example, the few students who have seriously read Robert Todd Lincoln's collection of his father's papers report interesting insights into immigration history, particularly from the Far West. Two isolated examples illustrate this point.[1] A certain Dr. William Rabé, representing Germans on the Pacific coast, repeatedly protests to Lincoln against the dominant influence of Colonel Edward Baker, transplanted Illinois Republican in Oregon, in appointments and patronage. Rabé points to the German support of Lincoln as spokesman for free labor and free homesteads in 1860, and asserts that the Germans are unhappy because they are not getting proper consideration in the distribution of Republican patronage in the West. From Texas, Anthony M.

[1] The Robert Todd Lincoln Collection, no. 19, William Rabé to Abraham Lincoln, San Francisco, 1 April 1861; no. 30, Anthony M. Dignowitz, "Memorial on Texas," 24 December 1861.

Dignowitz, physician and soldier, petitions somewhat tardily (24 December 1861) for military occupation of Texas in order to protect the loyal citizens of that state. Dignowitz claims that the Germans were invited to settle in Texas with the promise that Texas would become a free state. Sixty-five thousand German soldiers are now in the Union army, he adds, and Texas should be reconquered and transformed into a free state. What is more, Dignowitz submitted a plan of attack for this enterprise, which Lincoln in turn referred to the Committee on Military Affairs, and which the committee ordered printed. Dignowitz envisioned a two-pronged attack: one force striking north from Corpus Christi, the other overland from the Kansas border, and incidentally subduing the Indian Territory on the way. It would be flattering and congenial to the feelings of citizens of German origin, this amateur strategist points out, if part of these armies could be composed of German citizen-soldiers. Then when the state is reconquered, this force could be used against Louisiana and Arkansas. The West reconquered; slaves emancipated, loyal owners compensated, and all rebel property confiscated; Negroes colonized in Florida — Texas would be opened to great streams of immigration!

Mention of the Southwest and the Far West suggests a second significant need in immigration studies. The only historians to have dealt adequately with the role of immigration to the Far West are Kenneth O. Bjork, whose *West of the Great Divide* is a fresh and stimulating study of Norwegian immigration to the Pacific coast (alas, nothing similar has been done for any other ethnic group), and William Mulder, who has given us a scholarly account of the great Mormon migrations from Scandinavia.[2]

I submit another possibility for further immigration studies. This concerns nativism, that is, the intense opposition to an internal minority on the ground of its foreign or un-American connections and character. On the one hand a new investigation is needed into the origins and nature of the presuppositions that bring about nativism, and of

[2] Bjork, *West of the Great Divide: Norwegian Migration to the Pacific Coast, 1847–1893* (Northfield, Minn.: Norwegian-American Historical Association, 1958); Mulder, *Homeward to Zion: The Mormon Migration from Scandinavia* (Minneapolis: University of Minnesota Press, 1957).

the changes that these presuppositions undergo in each nativist episode. When we view the United States as a frontier of Europe, the possibility suggests itself that what is termed "American" by nativists might really be quite general ideas whose roots run deep into the traditions of Western civilization. We should undertake to trace the first outlines of the concepts that later crystallize into more elaborate patterns of thought. The investigation of nativist presuppositions will involve both analysis and synthesis.[3] We need a wider coverage of nativist materials, especially European, along with an analysis and synthesis of the major premises implicit in these materials. Such a study might reveal that there was not just a single pattern of nativist thought in America, but many — some dominant, others incipient or latent — and that these varied from individual to individual and from time to time.

Nativist opposition to or rejection of "foreign" groups was in fact a judgment on the nature and rights of man. Nativism is, therefore, by its own terms, a religious matter, since questions concerning the nature and destiny of man have theological implications. This opens up the possibility of further study of nativism as an aspect of religious thought significant in its own right.

Such an analytical approach would enable the historian to participate in interdisciplinary studies which break through the compartmentalized traditions of the American academy. Nativist tendencies and habits of mind might be illuminated by joint efforts with philosophers and theologians in getting at attitudes enmeshed in thought and feeling, and characteristic ideas that underpin them. The increasing role of theological studies in American universities, and recent symposia of historians, theologians, philosophers, and sociologists, help to create a climate favorable to such intellectual collaboration.

Another urgent need is to study immigration and nativism in terms of the structure of American society itself, to work out interrelations between classes and regions on the one hand and ethnic groups on the other. Only in this way can historians hope to understand the national and social characteristics that have shaped the relations

[3] John C. Greene, "Objectives and Methods in Intellectual History," *Mississippi Valley Historical Review*, 44:58–74 (June 1957).

between the various ethnic groups that go to make up the population of the United States.[4]

Both methods — the search for presuppositions of thought, and the study of the American social process in which competition for status in a mobile society changes social structure — could help discourage a conservative or nationalist emphasis on the writing and teaching of American history. Such approaches to the subject might discourage, too, the purely antiquarian collection of data without interpretation. As Philip Jordan said recently, "Social history must organize itself and most assuredly spend as much time . . . in interpretation as it does in collecting. Indeed, I am not sure but that the result would be salutary if a moratorium were declared on all new research and the time thus saved be devoted to understanding and bringing together what has already been written."[5]

Finally I recommend an intensification of the approach which Arnold Schrier has made in his fascinating study of *Ireland and the American Emigration, 1850–1900.*[6] As he states, American studies in the field of emigration-immigration have been heavily concentrated on the contributions made by European immigrants to American society, and little has been done to describe the impact of emigration on the country of origin. Certainly there is room for more investigation of American influences which filtered back to the Continent, along the lines suggested by Mr. Schrier. Substantial collections of letters, documents, and newspapers are available in the archives of private emigrant-aid societies in Europe, and it would not be difficult to obtain microfilms of these. I have in mind particularly the archival deposits of the Ludwig Missionsverein in Munich, the Leopoldinen Stiftung in Vienna, and the Society for the Propagation of the Faith in Fribourg. The holdings of some of the major nineteenth-century shipping firms are also a rich source, such as the Nord Deutscher Lloyd collection. So, too, the records of the national port authorities at ports of embarkation, and materials in

---

[4] John Higham, "Another Look at Nativism," *Catholic Historical Review*, 44:147–58 (July 1958).

[5] "Social History: A Nation Announcing Itself," *Ohio Historical Quarterly*, 66:237 (July 1957).

[6] Minneapolis: University of Minnesota Press, 1958.

emigrant-aid hostels — thus the Leo Haus near old Castle Garden in New York was a gold mine of primary documents, all faithfully and lovingly preserved.

New insights into the cultural-folkloristic patterns, as well as into the religious and economic realities of immigration, are thus possible with the exploitation of new materials. A beginning might be made in the public and private holdings in Germany, France, Switzerland, and Austria. When these are exhausted other rich fields beckon.

by THEODORE C. BLEGEN

The Saga of the Immigrant

THE newer emphasis upon the history of immigration has been forwarded in recent years by increasing concern about cultural and social forces in the national life, coupled with the emergence of trained scholars who found immigration, without the coloring of filiopietistic bias, an inviting and challenging research domain. They felt that the frontier hypothesis of Turner by no means explained the diversity in American customs and attitudes or revealed the full complexion of American culture, and that a new approach was needed.

The wide-ranging saga of the immigrant opened fresh avenues to the understanding of American history, though the newer school of scholars did not erect any single theory or hypothesis. American civilization is too complex to be comprehended through any one all-embracing interpretation or thesis. Scholars were interested in the interplay of Old World backgrounds of thought and practice with the New World environment, and were aware of processes of "acculturation," although they did not make much use, if any, of that impressive word. When, in 1922, Arthur M. Schlesinger published his *New Viewpoints in American History*, the first essay in his book included a sympathetic interpretation of "The Influence of Immigration on American History," and his opinion that "the two grand themes of American history" were "the influence of immigration upon American life and institutions, and the influence of the American environment, especially the frontier in the early days and the industrial

NOTE. This essay will appear in *Research Opportunities in American Cultural History*, the proceedings of a conference sponsored by Lilly Endowment, Inc., held at Washington University in October 1959, to be published in 1961 by the University of Kentucky Press. Used by permission of the University of Kentucky Press.

integration of more recent times, upon the ever-changing composite population." [1]

We are never far away from Turner, however, in our thinking about large forces in American history. He did not explore American immigration history carefully and critically; but early in his career — even before he wrote his famous frontier essay — he asserted that the story of the peopling of America had not yet been written. "We do not understand ourselves," he said, and in viewing the immigrants, he looked beyond their "bone and sinew" and realized that they "brought with them deeply inrooted customs and ideas." He believed that the American destiny was interwoven with theirs, and later he wrote, "We shall not understand the contemporary United States without studying immigration historically." It is fair to say that he viewed immigration, not merely as a recurring problem, as did many of his generation, but as a constant and significant factor in American history. In his major exposition of frontier influences, he paid very little attention to the impact of millions of immigrants, but in some degree he foreshadowed the newer school. [2]

We cannot write the history of American immigration without drawing upon diverse kinds of materials. The most baffling problem for the historian is to realize that immigrants are people, not nicely tabulated statistics, and that to understand people calls for the use of sources as varied and far-reaching as their interests and activities, their minds and emotions, their work and ambitions, their frustrations and happiness, their very lives.

Among the many sources that offer research possibilities for the study of immigration are the ballads and songs produced in great numbers and many languages by and about immigrants from the

[1] *New Viewpoints in American History* (New York: Macmillan, 1922), p. 2. See also Professor Schlesinger's revision of this essay under the title "The Role of the Immigrant" in his *Paths to the Present* (New York: Macmillan, 1949), pp. 51–76, with an excellent bibliographical note, pp. 286–89.

[2] Turner's essays on "The Significance of History" and "Problems in American History" are in *The Early Writings of Frederick Jackson Turner* (Madison: University of Wisconsin Press, 1938), pp. 63–64, 82. See also his articles in the *Chicago Record-Herald*, August 28, September 4, 11, 25, and October 16, 1901. Much of his later basic thinking is recorded in his "Middle Western Pioneer Democracy," *Minnesota History Bulletin*, 3:393–414 (August 1920).

European countries to the United States. An illustration may be found in "Oleana," with its satirical stanzas hailing Ole Bull's immigrant colony in Pennsylvania and describing America as the land where fantastic dreams came true — as indeed they did, though not precisely in the terms of this Scandinavian ballad from the 1850's. Across the waters from Norway, according to the song:

> They give you land for nothing in jolly Oleana,
> And grain comes leaping from the ground in floods
> of golden manna.

> And ale as strong and sweet as the best you've
> ever tasted,
> It's running in the foamy creek, where most of
> it is wasted.

> And little roasted piggies, with manners quite
> demure, Sir,
> They ask you, Will you have some ham? And then
> you say, Why, sure, Sir.[3]

Every country had such ballads, their gay irony not quite masking the essential truth of their claims. A Swedish song from the same period closes each of its many stanzas with the refrain:

> Isn't that impossible?
> Ah, but it is wonderful!
> Pity that America
> Is so far away!

Pity, indeed, for this was the picture:

> Trees that strike their roots in earth
> Sweet they are as sugar,
> Country full of maidens —
> Lovely dolls they are, Sir.

> Chicks and ducks come raining down,
> Steaming hot and tender,

[3] For the full verse translation of "Oleana," see Theodore C. Blegen, *Land of Their Choice: The Immigrants Write Home* (Minneapolis: University of Minnesota Press, 1955), pp. 282–83. The original text, with a prose translation and the music, appears in Blegen and Martin B. Ruud, *Norwegian Emigrant Songs and Ballads* (Minneapolis: University of Minnesota Press, 1936), pp. 187–98.

Fly upon your table,
Knives and forks in place, Sir.[4]

Such ballads remind us that the immigrant was a human being, and they also illustrate the fact that the sources for interpreting immigration are varied and are connected with literature, folklore, language, and music, as well as with sociology, economics, and politics. In my exploration of immigration sources, I have found the texts — in many instances the music — of more than a hundred emigrant ballads. I have noted with interest the use that John Kolehmainen has made of Finnish songs and ballads in his emigration studies.[5] More recently Arnold Schrier, writing about *Ireland and the American Emigration*, quotes Irish ballads, including the unhappy one of "Noreen Bawn," who sailed off

To that place where the Missouri
With the Mississippi flows.

She returned to Ireland, died, and her weeping mother sang

'Twas the shame of emigration
Laid you low, my Noreen Bawn.[6]

The emigrant ballads touch not only emigrant dreams of what America might be, but also homeland conditions, the reasons for emigration, farewells, the Atlantic voyage, and varied experiences — good and bad — in the New World. It is time to launch a cooperative hunt for such ballads in many languages, to translate them into English, to give them appropriate interpretation, and thus to make them available to students of American history and culture. The fruits of such a hunt would provide an addition to our folk literature and perhaps contribute new insight into the thoughts and emotions that accompanied the migrations which statisticians present in tables.

[4] Theodore C. Blegen, *Grass Roots History* (Minneapolis: University of Minnesota Press, 1947), pp. 43–44.

[5] See John I. Kolehmainen and George W. Hill, *Haven in the Woods* (Madison: State Historical Society of Wisconsin, 1951), and Blegen and Ruud, *Norwegian Emigrant Songs and Ballads*.

[6] Schrier, *Ireland and the American Emigration, 1850–1900* (Minneapolis: University of Minnesota Press, 1958), p. 99. In a chapter entitled "The Invisible Result: Cant and Custom," Mr. Schrier presents the texts of several other Irish emigrant ballads.

One of the weaknesses of filiopietists, alongside their parading of immigrant claims and their emphasis on heroes and "contributions," was their failure to search out rigorously the basic sources for the stories they wanted to tell. What they did is not without value, but their documentation was as inadequate as their methods were uncritical. We cannot deal responsibly with research opportunities in this field unless we give thought to primary sources and their availability, and here we need to be reminded that the history of American immigration is transatlantic, and indeed international in a broad sense. Sources, in abundant variety, are to be found in the Old World as well as in the New. Our subject is in no sense parochial.

Sources in the Old World need to be ferreted out not only because they are vital to the understanding of emigrant backgrounds and the impact of America on the Old World, but also because the story of immigration is richly recorded in contemporary letters that went back by the millions to home communities. Have they been preserved? Can they be found and used? To a surprising degree, the answer is Yes. Bundles of "America letters" are preserved by countless families in various European countries; and in some of those countries, including the Scandinavian, nineteenth-century newspapers printed vast numbers of letters reporting experiences, bright or dismal, in America — all this as part of spirited national debates on the merits of emigration, thus reflecting a pervasive European curiosity about the United States. The discovery of America did not end with Columbus.

Historical treasures have been garnered from such sources. A few years ago, in *Land of Their Choice*,[7] I brought together English translations of representative America letters found in Norway — letters having a nineteenth-century sweep from New York to California and from Minnesota to Texas. I did this partly because the story they unfolded was interesting, original, and significant, and in part because I wanted to forward a movement for gathering up and making available to students of American history similar letters from all

[7] In addition to *Land of Their Choice*, see *The America Letters* (Oslo: Norwegian Academy of Science, 1928), and "Early 'America Letters,'" in Theodore C. Blegen, *Norwegian Migration to America, 1825–1860* (Northfield, Minn.: Norwegian-American Historical Association, 1931), pp. 196–213.

countries in the Old World. With some of my friends, I have dreamed of a twenty-volume work covering a century of migration and bringing together in English translations America letters and diaries as preserved in all the countries of Europe. Perhaps the plan was over-ambitious. It has not been realized, but much has been done and more will be done. A scholar in Wales, Alan Conway, has made a collection of Welsh immigrant letters that offers substance for many community and state studies in the future.[8] American efforts, too, have encouraged the collecting of such sources in some of the European countries, especially the Scandinavian. An illustration is afforded by Norway, where a federation of local historical societies has for more than thirty years gathered up America letters for deposit in a national center for original historical sources.

The letters are a common people's diary, its interest heightened because the contemporary recorders were personally experiencing a change of worlds. They describe the physical migration in a thousand details; but as the reader follows the records through decades, he begins to realize, as William Mulder has observed, that "the immigrant crossed more than an ocean and a continent." His "traveling was

> . . . across the sprung longitudes of the mind
> And the blood's latitudes." [9]

We must not forget that the America letter was read by many people. The letters mirror the image of America formed in the minds of great numbers of Europeans. That image "was changing, and reflected kaleidoscopic scenes through decades when America was moving westward," and its quality is derived not only from "the external events recorded, but also from the changes mirrored in the thoughts and reactions of immigrants" through the years.[10] The letters are also

[8] *The Welsh in America: Letters from the Immigrants* (Minneapolis: University of Minnesota Press, 1961).

[9] See "Through Immigrant Eyes: Utah History at the Grass Roots," in *Utah Historical Quarterly*, January 1954, p. 41; and the same author's *Homeward to Zion: The Mormon Migration from Scandinavia* (Minneapolis: University of Minnesota Press, 1957), p. xi. The lines are quoted by Mr. Mulder from a poem by John Ciardi.

[10] Blegen, "The Immigrant Image of America," in *Land of Their Choice*, pp. 8–14 and (for the phrases quoted), pp. xi–xii. One of the best articles on the interest

of value for their detailed documentation of events and changes in the succession of frontiers where they originated.

It would be a mistake to leave the impression that immigrant letters constitute the only source that opens inviting opportunities for research. My own interest in the field began with a book of travel and description, Rynning's *True Account of America*, which I translated and edited many years ago.[11] I soon found myself deep in travel literature, archives, the immigrant press, memoirs, newspapers abroad, and a host of other sources, not omitting statistics. Much can be done with the historical use of European travel and observation in America, as Nevins, Commager, Handlin, and others have demonstrated in their anthologies. The immigrant press has been only lightly tapped for serious historical studies, in part because of linguistic obstacles, in part because newspaper files are widely scattered and often inaccessible. A national microfilm project is needed here, and its outlines were sketched at a conference held recently in Cleveland at the call of Carl Wittke, a leader in immigration research and writing. The immigrant newspaper press is a storehouse of source material for research in virtually all aspects of immigrant life in America in the nineteenth and twentieth centuries.

There has been much advance in immigration studies since Marcus Lee Hansen in 1927 described "Immigration as a Field for Historical Research."[12] That essay, in text and notes, still points the way to many special studies worth doing, especially in the area of community and group life, where, as the author believed, "the leaven in the lump can be detected." Hansen is rich in ideas and suggestions, but I shall not itemize them here since his article is well known and readily accessible. It would be enlightening, however, as a clue to research potentialities, to glance at work done since Hansen wrote his essay. Such a glance will serve as a guide not only to things done but also to comparable and related studies that might be attempted.

and value of America letters is George M. Stephenson, "When America Was the Land of Canaan," *Minnesota History*, 10:237–60 (September 1929).

[11] Minneapolis: Norwegian-American Historical Association, 1926. The original was published in Christiania, Norway, in 1838.

[12] *American Historical Review*, 32:500–18 (April 1927).

Hansen's career was cut off all too early, but in 1940 his three major books were published — *The Atlantic Migration, The Mingling of the Canadian and American Peoples*, and a volume of essays entitled *The Immigrant in American History*. Taken together they document his basic ideas, the sweep of his interest, his critical research, and his prescription, by scholarly example, of therapy for the filiopietists.

George Malcolm Stephenson, drawing upon Swedish sources, illustrated and interpreted America letters and also explored with acumen the religious aspects of immigration with reference to the Swedish migrants. Scholars interested in Norwegian migration have detailed European backgrounds and the American environmental experience in a long shelf of books, many of them documentary, which offer not a few suggestions of things that might be done for other immigrant groups. Carlton C. Qualey has written an illuminating study along the lines of flow and distribution — a kind of research that seemed highly important to Hansen.[13] Some of the many-faceted aspects of immigration research are illustrated in path-breaking works by Einar I. Haugen, Kenneth O. Bjork, Michael Kraus, and Henry A. Pochmann. They illuminate the linguistic interpretation of immigrant transition, the migration of professionally trained men, eighteenth-century parallels in the transit of culture, and the impact of German thought and literature upon America.[14]

In *West of the Great Divide* (1958), Dr. Bjork has given fresh illustrations of the historical value of the immigrant press as source material; and William Mulder has found and used abundant Mormon sources. Charlotte Erickson, exploring a quarter-century from 1860, has advanced knowledge of immigrant labor recruitment by American industry. New socio-historical approaches and substantial con-

[13] *Norwegian Settlement in the United States* (Northfield, Minn.: Norwegian-American Historical Association, 1938).

[14] Haugen, *The Norwegian Language in America: A Study in Bilingual Behavior* (2 vols.; Philadelphia: University of Pennsylvania Press, 1953); Bjork, *Saga in Steel and Concrete* (Northfield, Minn.: Norwegian-American Historical Association, 1947); Kraus, *The Atlantic Civilization: Eighteenth Century Origins* (Ithaca, N.Y.: Cornell University Press, 1949); Pochmann, *German Culture in America: Philosophical and Literary Influences, 1600–1900* (Madison: University of Wisconsin Press, 1957).

tributions in studies of immigrant urban experience have been made by Oscar Handlin in *Boston's Immigrants* (1941) and by Robert Ernst in *Immigrant Life in New York City, 1825–1863* (1949). Henry S. Lucas has uncovered rich treasures in immigrant memoirs and related sources for the story of the Netherlanders in America. For the Irish there are new scholarly works that are a far cry indeed from earlier writings in this field. Carl Wittke and Colman J. Barry have deepened our understanding of the German migration; John Kolehmainen and others have used varied sources for the history of the Finns in America; and the Jewish tercentenary has elicited a number of interesting and valuable studies.[15]

Merle Curti's *The Making of an American Community* (1959), though not primarily an immigration study, is a full-length exploration of the processes of acculturation in a single community. And this reminds me of a somewhat unusual essay on segregation and assimilation in a small Wisconsin community by the sociologist Peter A. Munch, which illustrates nicely the wedding of sociological and historical methods.[16] Nativism is a recurring phenomenon in American

[15] In addition to the titles specially mentioned in this paragraph, see Charlotte Erickson, *American Industry and the European Immigrant, 1860–1885* (Cambridge, Mass.: Harvard University Press, 1957); Henry S. Lucas, *Netherlanders in America: Dutch Immigration to the United States and Canada, 1789–1950* (Ann Arbor: University of Michigan Press, 1955), and *Dutch Immigrant Memoirs and Related Writings* (2 vols.; Assen, Netherlands: Van Gorcum, 1955); Carl F. Wittke, *The Irish in America* (Baton Rouge: Louisiana State University Press, 1956); James P. Shannon, *Catholic Colonization on the Western Frontier* (New Haven: Yale University Press, 1957); Sister M. Justille McDonald, *History of the Irish in Wisconsin* (Washington, D.C.: Catholic University of America Press, 1954); Wittke, *Refugees of Revolution: The German Forty-Eighters in America* (Philadelphia: University of Pennsylvania Press, 1952) and *The German Language Press in America* (Lexington: University of Kentucky Press, 1957); Colman J. Barry, *The Catholic Church and German Americans* (Milwaukee: Bruce, 1953); Oscar Handlin, *Adventure in Freedom: Three Hundred Years of Jewish Life in America* (New York: McGraw-Hill, 1954); Rufus Learsi, *The Jews in America: A History* (Cleveland and New York: World, 1954); and W. Gunther Plaut, *The Jews in Minnesota* (New York: American Jewish Historical Society, 1959). Since the preparation of this paper an excellent book on *Finnish Immigrants in America, 1880–1920*, by A. William Hoglund, has been published by the University of Wisconsin Press (Madison, 1960).

[16] Munch, "Segregation and Assimilation of Norwegian Settlements in Wisconsin," in *Norwegian-American Studies and Records* (Northfield, Minn.), 18:102–40 (1954).

life and politics; interest in this field is not of recent origin, but several notable contributions have appeared lately, especially by Ray A. Billington, John Higham, and Robert A. Divine; and Barbara Solomon has done brilliant interpretive work in her historical analysis of "ancestors and immigrants" in a New England setting.[17] A significant trend, definitely influenced by the newer school of immigration historians in the United States, is the increasing attention now being devoted to the impact of migration upon the home countries. A half-dozen books have appeared within recent years relating to English, Irish, and Scandinavian backgrounds, and the distinguished Norwegian historian Halvdan Koht has written a wide-ranging interpretation of *The American Spirit in Europe* (1949), with "a comprehensive view of the effect of American activities, struggles, and efforts upon European life and progress." [18]

I mention these writers and books, not with any thought of offering an inclusive bibliography, but as instances of significant work. The time may come when there will be a master synthesis of the history of American immigration, but, like the great American novel, this may prove an unrealized and unrealizable dream. Dr. Stephenson's *History of American Immigration* (1926), though a pioneering effort, was limited largely to immigration "as a factor in American political development." *We Who Built America* (1939) by Dr. Wittke brought together in a large frame the results of hundreds of studies up to that time; and in 1951 Handlin presented an

[17] Billington, *The Protestant Crusade, 1800–1860* (New York: Macmillan, 1938); Higham, *Strangers in the Land* (New Brunswick, N.J.: Rutgers University Press, 1955); Divine, *American Immigration Policy, 1924–1952* (New Haven: Yale University Press, 1957); Solomon, *Ancestors and Immigrants: A Changing New England Tradition* (Cambridge, Mass.: Harvard University Press, 1956).

[18] Wilbur S. Shepperson, *British Emigration to North America: Projects and Opinions in the Early Victorian Period* (Oxford: Blackwell; Minneapolis: University of Minnesota Press, 1957); Rowland T. Berthoff, *British Immigrants in Industrial America, 1790–1950* (Cambridge, Mass.: Harvard University Press, 1953); C. K. Yearley, *Britons in American Labor (1820–1914)* (Baltimore: Johns Hopkins Press, 1957); Brinley Thomas, *Migration and Economic Growth* (Cambridge, Eng.: Cambridge University Press, 1954); Arnold Schrier, *Ireland and the American Emigration, 1850–1900* (Minneapolis: University of Minnesota Press, 1958); Richard H. Heindel, *The American Impact on Great Britain, 1898–1914* (Philadelphia: University of Pennsylvania Press, 1940); Ingrid Semmingsen, *Veien mot Vest* [The Way West] (2 vols.; Oslo: Aschehoug, 1941, 1950).

eloquent interpretation in *The Uprooted*. We have still not achieved the great synthesis, however. Louis Adamic made some effort in this direction, but his approach was a reversion to the indignant and defensive mood and to the parading of claims. His *A Nation of Nations* (1945) is described by the historian of immigrant historiography as "virtually a glossary of the errors committed by the amateur investigators of immigrant history." [19]

If the great work seems remote, many lesser contributions are attainable. We need more area and group studies both for this country and for Canada — searches for "the leaven in the lump," with the use of interdisciplinary techniques. There is room for extensive additions to the edited letters, diaries, reports, memoirs, across the land and for many elements. We have all too little on the organizational life of immigrants. Henry Pochmann's recent book suggests the need for more studies in literature, thought, and art, both as to the impact of European cultural influence on America and as to immigrant creative work — and I recall that for the Norwegians alone I once made up a list of about a hundred immigrant novels that had never been turned into English, and perhaps do not deserve translation, but are of cultural historical interest. We need more studies of the immigrant in the urban community, and we need to reappraise the immigrant factor in the history of the American frontier. Immigrant social and intellectual life is rich in research possibilities. Inevitably migration, settlement, and the saga of people and the land as mirrored in fiction by Rölvaag's *Giants in the Earth* have attracted much attention, but many of the more genial and urbane aspects of immigrant transition invite research. Here, for instance, Henriette Koren Naeseth has given an illustration of illuminating work worth doing for many nationalities in her monograph on the pioneer Swedish theatei

[19] Edward N. Saveth, "The Immigrant in American History," in *Commentary*, 2:180–85 (August 1946). See also Dr. Saveth's valuable *American Historians and European Immigrants, 1875–1925* (New York: Columbia University Press, 1948). Since this paper was written, Maldwyn Allen Jones has published a compact single-volume history of *American Immigration*, Chicago History of American Civilization series (Chicago: University of Chicago Press, 1960). This is a useful survey, notable less for new research or fresh viewpoints and interpretations than for its objective handling of the story and its selective bibliography of American immigration.

and drama in Chicago.[20] Emigration and immigration as described and interpreted in novels, plays, and short stories by authors in both the Old and New worlds invite the critical appraisal of historians who are not committed to mere quantitative techniques, but have an eye to those imaginative approaches that give new and readier understanding. We need to see Hans and Olaf, Pierre, Guiseppe, and Patrick as human beings, emigrants and immigrants, persons who are born, work, live, love, and die, moving with their material and cultural baggage from one world to another, changing in their ways and attitudes as their worlds change, and having impact on the societies they left and on those with which they merged their lives.

There are inviting opportunities in immigrant church history, education, the story of the press, folklore and folk arts, sports and amusements, labor and industry, the emigrant trade, the story of the immigrant second generation (to which the novelist Rölvaag gave attention after writing *Giants in the Earth*), the immigrant farm and farm community, politics, the migration of culture in its grass-roots sense, and the European backgrounds of ideas and institutions. We need more studies of the emigrants who, successful or unsuccessful in America, returned to their homeland, and here Theodore Saloutos, in his research on the Greeks who went back to Greece, has pioneered new paths.[21] We urgently need critical and thoroughgoing studies of many national elements that have not yet found historians of high scholarly quality, and this need is particularly compelling for the immigrants from the southern and southeastern parts of Europe, from Latin America, and from the vast world to the Far East. We need more emphasis than we have had on the recent periods of immigration. Interesting and illuminating for the full saga would be a pictorial history of American immigration. Rich illustrative materials are now available in such institutions as the Library of Congress, the Nebraska and Minnesota historical societies, the George Eastman House in Rochester, New York, and various college and special museums and libraries.

[20] *The Swedish Theatre of Chicago, 1868–1950* (Chicago: Augustana College Library, 1951).

[21] *They Remember America: The Story of the Repatriated Greek-Americans* (Berkeley and Los Angeles: University of California Press, 1956).

There is need, also, of viewing the migration both of people and of ideas in world-wide compass — migration from the Old World to the New not only, but back and forth in many parts of the world in this jostling, restless age. Nor is the migration merely that from country to country — my own studies have indicated a close relationship of emigration and extensive internal migration in the countries that poured emigrants into America in the nineteenth and twentieth centuries. The problems both of world migration and of internal shifts in the countries of the Old World are too great and complex for treatment by our own historians alone. Scholars in many countries must cooperate if they are to deal adequately with the phenomenon of population movements in a vastly larger context than that simply of the immigrant influx into the United States.

The Hansen essay and the many books and innumerable articles that have appeared in the past two or three decades offer many other clues to research needed before we can fill out the general picture with large surveys and interpretations. As in other areas of cultural history, guides to source materials can aid scholars in their own hunts for unused or little-used records and can mark out potential paths to new subjects of research. Scholars for the most part are their own pathfinders, but they do not spurn assistance. Now and then we fail to appreciate the richness of sources already collected and available. An illustration is afforded by Homer L. Calkin in an article that describes the research materials in the National Archives on Irish immigration and naturalization, the political significance of the Irish in America, their social and economic conditions, their relations with the homeland, and various other topics.[22] In the realm of printed materials, O. F. Ander has made available an impressive list of selected references on the cultural heritage of the Swedish immigrant which reveals how ample and varied the historical documentation can be for a single element in the population.[23]

The problem of publication confronts all scholars, in whatever field. Many major works on immigration have been brought out

[22] "The United States Government and the Irish," *Irish Historical Studies*, 9:28–52 (March 1954).

[23] *The Cultural Heritage of the Swedish Immigrant. Selected References* (Rock Island, Ill.: Augustana College Library, 1956).

through university and other presses; and numerous articles have appeared in national and regional journals and in the organs of societies that focus their interest upon particular immigrant groups. How extended the opportunities are for essays and short documentary items even in the history of a single population element finds illustration in the work of the Norwegian-American Historical Association, which has published no fewer than twenty volumes of *Studies and Records* (and more than a score of other books) since it was founded in 1925.[24] Valuable as such contributions are for the national story, the importance of the total field and the mounting interest of American and European scholars suggest that the time may not be distant when a "Journal of Immigration" should be inaugurated. Such a journal could serve the useful purpose of bringing together general and special articles dealing with the immigrant in American life. Its special field could be that of American immigration from colonial times to the present, with due attention to Old World backgrounds and repercussions, but it could also grapple with emigration in its world-wide dimensions. Edited in accordance with rigorous critical standards, it could provide a forum for contributions that, by virtue of present circumstances, too often are restricted to narrow circles of readers. It could provide national and international encouragement to scholarship on the immigrant theme by bringing together studies of many areas, periods, elements, and problems. I do not doubt that, if a journal of such character came into being, scholars would provide it with rich content and competent editorial direction, with attention to good writing as well as to scholarly excellence.

[24] For an appraisal of the Association, see Franklin D. Scott, "Controlled Scholarship and Productive Nationalism," *Norwegian-American Studies and Records* (Northfield, Minn.), 17:130–48 (1952).

BIBLIOGRAPHY AND INDEX

About the Authors

FATHER COLMAN J. BARRY, O.S.B., is associate professor of history at St. John's University, Collegeville. While working toward the Ph.D. at the Catholic University of America, he did research in materials relating to immigration in European depositories as Penfield Fellow in 1950–51. He has written several books, including *The Catholic Church and German Americans*, and is editor of the *American Benedictine Review*.

THEODORE C. BLEGEN has contributed to the field of immigration studies as teacher and author for more than four decades. His writings and career are dealt with elsewhere in this volume.

HENRY STEELE COMMAGER, professor of history and American Studies at Amherst College and adjunct professor at Columbia, has written extensively on various aspects of American history. Two of his best known publications are *The Growth of the American Republic* (with Samuel E. Morison) and *The American Mind*. He is also editor of a 40-volume work in process, *The Rise of the American Nation*. Professor Commager has lectured at many universities both in the United States and abroad and has traveled widely.

JOHN T. FLANAGAN has been at the University of Illinois, where he is professor of English, since 1946. The author of more than sixty articles that have appeared in literary, historical, and critical journals, he has also written several books, of which the most recent are *The American Way*, *Folklore in American Literature*, and *American Literature, A College Survey* (with Clarence A. Brown). Professor Flanagan has been a Fulbright lecturer in both France and Belgium and a visiting professor in Japan.

OSCAR HANDLIN, director of the Center for the Study of the History of Liberty in America at Harvard University, is known in the United States and Europe as teacher, author, and lecturer. His first book, *Boston's Immigrants*, and his latest, *Immigration as a Factor in American History*, are only two of the many books and articles in which Professor Handlin has concerned himself with the subject of immigration. His *The Uprooted* won the Pulitzer Prize in 1951. He is also one of the editors of the *Harvard Guide to American History*.

PHILIP D. JORDAN is professor of history at the University of Minnesota. A native of Iowa, he took his undergraduate work at Northwestern University and his graduate training at the University of Iowa. His books include *Ohio Comes of Age, Singin' Yankees, The National Road, William Salter: Western Torchbearer,* and *The People's Health*; he has also contributed many articles to professional journals. Professor Jordan has long been specially interested in American social history.

HENRY A. POCHMANN is the author of the chapters on non-English writing in the United States appearing in *Literary History of the United States*. Books in which he has considered immigration history include *New England Transcendentalism and St. Louis Hegelianism, Bibliography of German Culture in America to 1940,* and *German Culture in America, 1600–1900* (which won the Loubat Prize of Columbia University). He is professor of American literature at the University of Wisconsin.

CARLTON C. QUALEY, professor of American history and chairman of the department of history at Carleton College, is preparing a history of European migration to the United States since 1815. He is the author of *Norwegian Settlement in the United States* and numerous articles on immigration history, including "Some Aspects of European Migration to the United States" in *Essays in American Historiography in Honor of Allan Nevins*, edited by D. Sheehan and H. C. Syrett.

FRANKLIN D. SCOTT, professor of history at Northwestern University, has long been interested in the problems of migration and cultural interchange, and has carried on and guided research in this field. He has traveled and studied repeatedly in the Scandinavian countries, the area of his primary concern. Among his books are *The United States and Scandinavia* and *The American Experience of Swedish Students*, a study undertaken for the Social Science Research Council.

INGRID SEMMINGSEN of Oslo, Norway, is noted especially for her two-volume work *Veien mot Vest*, a study of Norwegian emigration to America from 1825 to 1915. She has also published a history of the United States, *En Verdensmakt Blir Til*. Her latest work is an edited volume of cotters' recollections, *Husmannsminner*. Mrs. Semmingsen holds the doctorate in philosophy from the University of Oslo, has lectured extensively in that university, and has served on the Norwegian staff at the United Nations in New York.

Theodore C. Blegen: A Bibliography

I. Books and Pamphlets Related to Immigration

THIS list includes books written or edited by Mr. Blegen which relate in whole or in part to the history of immigration. In addition he was managing editor of publications of the Norwegian-American Historical Association from 1925 to 1960 (41 volumes).

Ole Rynning's True Account of America. Minneapolis: Norwegian-American Historical Association, 1926. 100 pages. Translated and edited.

Peter Testman's Account of His Experiences in North America. Northfield, Minn.: Norwegian-American Historical Association, 1927. 60 pages. Translated and edited.

The America Letters. Oslo: Norwegian Academy of Science, 1928. 25 pages.

Norwegian Migration to America, 1825–1860. Northfield, Minn.: Norwegian-American Historical Association, 1931. 413 pages.

The Civil War Letters of Hans Christian Heg. Northfield, Minn.: Norwegian-American Historical Association, 1936. 260 pages.

Norwegian Emigrant Songs and Ballads (with Martin B. Ruud). Minneapolis: University of Minnesota Press, 1936. 350 pages.

Norwegian Migration to America: The American Transition. Northfield, Minn.: Norwegian-American Historical Association, 1940. 655 pages. One section, *John Quincy Adams and the Sloop "Restoration,"* separately published, 1940. 29 pages.

Grass Roots History. Minneapolis: University of Minnesota Press, 1947. 266 pages.

Frontier Parsonage: The Letters of Olaus Fredrik Duus, Norwegian Pastor in Wisconsin, 1855–1858. Northfield, Minn.: Norwegian-American Historical Association, 1947. 120 pages. Edited; translations by the Verdandi Study Club of Minneapolis.

Frontier Mother: The Letters of Gro Svendsen. Northfield, Minn.: Norwegian-American Historical Association, 1950. 153 pages. Translated and edited with Pauline Farseth.

Land of Their Choice: The Immigrants Write Home. Minneapolis: University of Minnesota Press, 1955. 463 pages. Norwegian edition, *Amerikabrev.* Oslo: Aschehoug, 1959. 408 pages. Foreword by Ingrid Semmingsen.

NOTE. Based on a compilation by Zephyra E. Shepherd.

II. A Selected List of Articles and Documents
on Immigration

"The Historical Records of the Scandinavians in America," *Minnesota History Bulletin*, 2:413–18 (May 1918).

"The Competition of the Northwestern States for Immigrants," *Wisconsin Magazine of History*, 3:3–29 (September 1919).

"The Early Norwegian Press in America," *Minnesota History Bulletin*, 3:506–18 (November 1920).

"Colonel Hans Christian Heg," *Wisconsin Magazine of History*, 4:140–65 (December 1920).

"Cleng Peerson and Norwegian Immigration," *Mississippi Valley Historical Review*, 7:303–31 (March 1921).

"The Scandinavian Element and Agrarian Discontent," American Historical Association *Annual Report*, 1921, p. 219. An abstract.

"A Typical 'America Letter,' " *Mississippi Valley Historical Review*, 9:68–75 (June 1922).

"Official Encouragement of Immigration to Minnesota during the Territorial Period," *Minnesota History Bulletin*, 5:167–203 (August 1923). With Livia Appel.

"The Norwegian Government and the Early Norwegian Emigration," *Minnesota History*, 6:115–40 (June 1925).

"Norwegians in the West in 1844," *Norwegian-American Studies and Records*, 1:110–25 (1926).

"Minnesota's Campaign for Immigrants" and "Illustrative Documents," *Swedish Historical Society of America Yearbook*, 11:3–28, 11:29–83 (1926).

"Den norske utvandring som den gjenspeiler sig i sange og digte," *Nordmandsforbundet*, April 1929, pp. 109–12.

"Guri Endreson, Frontier Heroine," *Minnesota History*, 10:425–30 (December 1929).

"California Gull og Brasiliansk Kolonisajon," *Nordmandsforbundet* (Oslo), Christmas annual 1930, pp. 45–48.

"An Early Norwegian Settlement in Canada," Canadian Historical Association *Annual Report*, 1930, pp. 83–88.

"Immigrant Women and the American Frontier," *Norwegian-American Studies and Records*, 5:14–29 (1930).

"Leaders in American Immigration," Illinois Historical Society *Transactions*, 1931, pp. 145–55.

"Cleng Peerson," in *Dictionary of American Biography*, XIV, 390. New York: Scribner, 1934. Other articles in volumes of this series on Ole Rynning, Johan R. Reiersen, Norwegian Immigration, Oleana.

"An Official Report on Norwegian and Swedish Immigration, 1870," *Norwegian-American Studies and Records*, 13:46–65 (1943).

"The Ballad of Oleana," *Common Ground*, 5:73–77 (Autumn 1944).

"Behind the Scenes of Emigration: A Series of Letters from the 1840's," *Norwegian-American Studies and Records*, 14:78–116 (1944).

"An Immigrant Exploration of the Middle West in 1839," *Norwegian-American Studies and Records*, 14:41–53 (1944).

"The Saga of Saga Hill," *Minnesota History*, 29:289–299 (December 1948).

"The Second Twenty-Five Years," *Norwegian-American Studies and Records*, 17:149–58 (1952).

BIBLIOGRAPHY

"Adventures in Historical Research," *Wisconsin Magazine of History*, 39:3–6, 47–48 (Autumn 1955).

"The Immigrant Image of America," *Norwegian-American Studies and Records*, 19:1–14 (1956).

"The America Book," *Illinois History*, 12:145–47 (March 1959).

"Singing Immigrants and Pioneers," in Joseph J. Kwiat and Mary C. Turpie, eds., *Studies in American Culture*. Minneapolis: University of Minnesota Press, 1959. Pp. 171–88.

III. Some Books and Pamphlets in Other Fields

A Report on the Public Archives. Madison: State Historical Society of Wisconsin, 1918. 115 pages.

The Unfinished Autobiography of Henry Hastings Sibley, Together with a Selection of Hitherto Unpublished Letters from the Thirties. Minneapolis: Voyageur Press, 1932.

Minnesota: Its History and Its People — A Study Outline. Minneapolis: University of Minnesota Press, 1937. 237 pages. Assisted by Lewis Beeson.

Building Minnesota. Boston: Heath, 1938. 450 pages.

Readings in Early Minnesota History. Minneapolis: University of Minnesota, 1938. 286 pages. Mimeographed.

Lincoln in World Perspective. Northfield, Minn.: Carleton College, 1943. 12 pages.

Horace William Shaler Cleveland: Pioneer American Landscape Architect. St. Paul: St. Anthony Park Area Historical Association, 1949. 13 pages.

The Land Lies Open. Minneapolis: University of Minnesota Press, 1949. 246 pages.

With Various Voices: Recordings of North Star Life, 1654–1900. St. Paul: Itasca Press, 1949. 380 pages. Edited with Philip D. Jordan.

The Preparation of College Teachers. Washington, D.C.: American Council on Education, 1950. 186 pages. Edited with Russell M. Cooper.

The Crowded Box-Room. La Crosse, Wis.: Sumac Press, 1951. 49 pages.

Sherlock Holmes: Master Detective. La Crosse, Wis.: Sumac Press, 1952. 86 pages. Edited with E. W. McDiarmid.

Lincoln's Imagery, A Study in Word Power. La Crosse, Wis.: Sumac Press, 1954. 32 pages.

Book Collecting and Scholarship. Minneapolis: University of Minnesota Press, 1954. 67 pages. With James F. Bell, Stanley Pargellis, Colton Storm, and Louis B. Wright.

The Harvests of Knowledge: A Report on Research Potentials and Problems in the State University of New York. Albany: Research Foundation of the State University of New York, 1957. 48 pages.

Exploring Sherlock Holmes. La Crosse, Wis.: Sumac Press, 1957. 123 pages. Edited with E. W. McDiarmid.

Minnesota History: A Guide to Reading and Study. Minneapolis: University of Minnesota Press, 1960. 223 pages. With Theodore L. Nydahl.

IV. A Selected List of Articles in Fields Other Than Immigration

"James Wickes Taylor: A Biographical Sketch," *Minnesota History Bulletin*, 1:153–219 (November 1915).

"A Plan for the Union of British North America and the United States," *Mississippi Valley Historical Review*, 4:470–83 (March 1918).

"Minnesota Pioneer Life as Revealed in Newspaper Advertisements," *Minnesota History*, 7:99–121 (June 1926).

"Campaigning with Seward in 1860," *Minnesota History*, 8:150–71 (June 1927).

"Some Aspects of Historical Work under the New Deal," *Mississippi Valley Historical Review*, 21:195–206 (September 1934).

"Fort St. Charles and the Northwest Angle," *Minnesota History*, 18:231–48 (September 1937).

"The 'Fashionable Tour' on the Upper Mississippi," *Minnesota History*, 20:377–96 (December 1939).

"Two Missionaries in the Sioux Country," *Minnesota History*, 21:15–32, 158–75, 272–83 (March, June, September 1940).

"Pioneer Bookshelves and Modern Libraries," *Minnesota History*, 22:351–66 (December 1941).

"Armistice and War on the Minnesota Frontier," *Minnesota History*, 24:11–25 (March 1943).

"Hospitals on the Western Frontier," *Hospitals* (Chicago), 17:73–75 (August 1943); 17:70–72 (September 1943).

"Our Widening Province," *Mississippi Valley Historical Review*, 31:3–20 (June 1944). Presidential address, Mississippi Valley Historical Association.

"The Graduate School in the Land-Grant Colleges and Universities," Association of Land-Grant Colleges and Universities *Proceedings*, 1944, pp. 189–94.

"Fundamentals of Graduate Education," *Journal of Dental Education*, 10:181–92 (April 1946).

"The Graduate Schools and the Education of College Teachers," *Educational Record*, 29:12–25 (January 1948).

"Training Leadership for Tomorrow," *Social Service Review*, 24:319–26 (September 1950).

"Ferment in Graduate Education," *National Education Journal*, 39:685–86 (December 1950).

"A Scholar Looks at Inter-Library Cooperation," *Library Quarterly*, 22:13–17 (January 1952).

"A Movement Gains Momentum," *School and Society*, 75:17–20 (January 12, 1952).

"Toward a Common Front," *School and Society*, 76:161–67 (September 13, 1952).

"The University in Crisis — Fidelity to Trust," *Minnesota Alumni*, 52:5–8, 31 (May–June 1953).

"The Halls of Science and American Research," *Minnesota Chemist*, 5:7–11, 22 (November–December 1953).

"The Prospect for the Liberal Arts," *Quarterly Journal of Speech*, 45:388–92 (December 1954). Reprinted in *Thoughts on the Humanities*. Washington, D.C.: American Council of Learned Societies, 1955.

"The Potential of Home Economics in Education and the Community," *Journal of Home Economics*, 47:479–82 (September 1955).

"A Century of Manuscript Collecting," *Minnesota History*, 34:337–40 (Winter 1955).

"Graduate Education and Research: Problems and Prospects," *Graduate School Record* (Ohio State University), 11(no. 3):3–7 (December 1957).

"Trustees of the Centennial Heritage," in R. M. Cooper, *The Two Ends of the Log*. Minneapolis: University of Minnesota Press, 1958. Pp. 293–302.

BIBLIOGRAPHY

"How Can Graduate Schools Increase the Supply of College Teachers?" *Journal of Higher Education*, 30:127–33 (March 1959).

"Some Thoughts on the Nature and Meaning of Scholarship," *Medical Bulletin* (Minnesota Medical Foundation), 31:89–93 (November 1, 1959).

"What's Past Is Prologue," in *Minnesota Heritage*. Minneapolis: Denison, 1960. Pp. 2–9.

"Education Must Liberate Man . . . and Make Him Humane," *Minnesota Journal of Education*, 41(no. 1):16–17 (September 1960).

Index

INDEX

INDEX

Methodist church, in Norway, 39
Metropolitan Record, New York, 67
Migration, internal, immigration throws light on, 11–12, 13–14, 18
Migration and Economic Growth, Thomas, 128
Mingling of the Canadian and American Peoples, The, Hansen, 146
Moberg, Vilhelm, 5, 82
Moby Dick, Melville, 80
Möllhausen, Heinrich B., 81
Morris, Wright, 91
Mortgage Your Heart, Winther, 87
Motley, Willard, 94
Mulder, Arnold, 83
Mulder, William, 144, 146
Munch, Peter A., 147
Muskego Manifesto, *1845,* 35
My American Pilgrimage, Christowe, 85
My Ántonia, Cather, 5, 85, 91

Nabokov, Vladimir, 93
Naeseth, Henriette K., 149
Nation of Nations, A, Adamic, 149
National character, American, 68–79
Nationalism, 4–5
Native Son, Wright, 94
Nativism, 4, 14, 64–66: study of, 135–37, 147. *See also* Know-Nothing party, Religion and immigration, Restrictions on immigration
Netherlands, emigration from studied, 147
Nevins, Allan, 133, 145
New York Public Library, immigration materials, 127
Newspapers: effect of American papers in Norway, 41–42; effect of American papers in England, 42n21, 49; as sources for immigration study, 128–29, 145
Nord Deutscher Lloyd, 137
Norway, emigration from, 34–47 *passim,* 117: studied, 115, 135
Norwegian-American Historical Association, publications, 7, 115, 152
Norwegian-American liberal associations, 38
Norwegian-American press, 41–42
Norwegian census of *1920,* shows returned emigrants, 44
Norwegian-Danish Evangelical Lutheran Church in America, 61n15
Norwegian influence in U.S., studied, 108

Norwegians in fiction, 81–95 *passim,* 149

O Pioneers! Cather, 87
Occupation, effect of immigration on, 18, 124
"Oleana," folk song quoted, 141
O'Neill, Eugene, 112
Ostenso, Martha, 82, 83
Owen, Robert, 109

Pagano, Jo, 83
Philosophy, German influence in, 109, 111
Pnin, Nabokov, 93
Pochmann, Henry A., 126
Poland, emigration from, 102
Polish Peasant in Europe and America, Thomas and Znaniecki, 129
Politics and immigration, 3: in Norway, 33, 37–40; in England, 49–50; in Ireland, 50
Poole, Ernest, 83
Poor Hater, The, Ready, 89
Population, foreign, U.S., *1790,* 101
Porter, William Sydney (O. Henry), 21
Positive Contribution by Immigrants, The, UNESCO, 105
Postl, Karl, 81
Pound, Ezra, 109, 113
Primitive, The, Manfred, 89
Pritchard, John, 108
Progress and Poverty, George, 93
Progressivism, 3–5
Promised Land, The, Antin, 5, 90
Pudd'nhead Wilson, Clemens, 80
Puritanism, 13–14, 110–11

Qualey, Carlton C., 146
Quick, Herbert, 83
"Quota system," 8–9

Rabé, Dr. William, 134
Races and Immigrants in America, Commons, 4
Ready, William, 89
Regional differences, U.S., 74–77
Religion and immigration, 15, 39, 122: prejudice against immigrants, 64–66. *See also* Church of the Latter-day Saints, Puritanism, Society for the Propagation of the Faith
Religious Aspects of Swedish Immigration, Stephenson, 39
Remittances, from emigrants to homeland, 100, 103, 130